I0449582

A Call to Peace: A Guide to Christian Pacifism and Peacemaking

Brendan Joseph O'Dea

Copyright © 2016 Brendan Joseph O'Dea

All rights reserved, including the right to reproduce this book, or portions thereof in any form. No part of this text may be reproduced, transmitted, downloaded, decompiled, reverse engineered, or stored, in any form or introduced into any information storage and retrieval system, in any form or by any means, whether electronic or mechanical without the express written permission of the author.

The views expressed in this work are solely those of the author and do not necessarily reflect the views of the publisher, and the publisher hereby disclaims any responsibility for them.

ISBN: 978-1-326-87426-1

PublishNation
www.publishnation.co.uk

*To my wife Rositsa for all her encouragement,
to JC, KC and JR for their advice and assistance,
and to my family for their support*

'And they shall beat their swords into plowshares,
And their spears into pruning hooks:
Nation shall not lift up sword against nation,
Neither shall they learn war anymore.'
(Isaiah 2:4)

'Blessed are the peacemakers, for they shall be called the
Children of God.'
(Matthew: 5:9)

'Injustice anywhere is a threat to justice everywhere.'
(Martin Luther King)

'There will be peace on earth when there is peace among the
world religions.'
(Hans Kung)

Contents

Introduction   ix

Chapter 1: History   1

Chapter 2: Methods   18

Chapter 3: People   23

Chapter 4: Organisations   68

Chapter 5: Conclusion   96

Notes   99

Bibliography   109

Appendices (Lists of Profiled People / Organisations)   115

Introduction

I wrote this short book because I believe it is important that Christianity, along with all other major religions, presents itself as an agent of peace rather than one of division or conflict. I hope to show that Christianity can uncompromisingly embrace this role and that it is stronger and more appealing for it. This is all the more urgent due to a general perception of Christianity in the opposite light. It is vital that Christianity, and religion in general, promotes peaceful co-existence; good religion should be the embodiment of peace. Pacifism should be not just a reaction to the threat of war but a lived way of life. Due to their pacifist principles, religious groups such as the Quakers have always been prominent in peace movements. I have chosen to focus on Christianity because this is the tradition that has shaped my own views, but one of the major themes throughout the book is the need for interfaith dialogue to foster co-operation between religions and to overcome divisions between them. Christianity is not a homogenous entity and there will always be groups and individuals at the margins who are unwilling to co-operate with others and who delight in spreading discord. It is possible that pacifism and peacemaking could serve as a link to unite highly divergent theological elements within the Christian faith. There are many people of goodwill prepared to promote a peaceful, if diverse, Christianity. Diversity is not a bad thing and can offer many varied and enlightening perspectives. However, due to the amount of internecine conflict between various Christian groups over the centuries, working together for the promotion of peace could serve as a unifying force. Sectarianism has no place in a global Christianity, or any other major religion, and it should be possible to agree to differ, while at the same time co-operating for the greater good.

I will look at Christian pacifism in general, as well as introducing individual Christian peacemakers, who may or may not consider themselves pacifist. This is a broad field and my examination is by no means comprehensive. While this is not an academic book, I will still provide references to give due credit and to point the reader to additional sources they may find useful. I will start by looking at the development of Christianity, to try to understand why in some contexts it has promoted peace and in other situations provoked conflict. I will look at some individuals who have adopted a peaceful stance from a Christian perspective, sometimes bucking against the institutional churches in the process. I will examine the methods used to further peace and justice, before outlining some Christian organisations involved in promoting pacifism and peacemaking. I am not trying to say that individuals should always be peaceful just because they are religious or Christian. This would be too high an ideal to aspire to. But if they are not peaceful, they should not try to justify this through reference to their faith. However, faiths themselves should always inspire peaceful ideals.

1. History:

'Blessed are the peacemakers: for they shall be called the Children of God'.

(Matthew 5:9)

The above line is from the Beatitudes, delivered by Jesus as part of the Sermon on the Mount, exhorting us to live lives that are peaceful, meek and merciful. It provides a promising basis for the development of a Christianity that is wholly peaceful and we must ask ourselves how we got from this starting point to where the churches are today. However, we must remember that the Bible represents a canon of diverse writings from varied sources written over a long period of time and for every biblical quote that can be found to justify one perspective, there is equally likely to be a quote that appears to support the opposite. Even if we are committed to a particular religious tradition, it may be wise to ensure our views are formed not just by that tradition and its scriptures, but also by other factors such as personal experience, reason, intuition and our wider spiritual outlook. It is not a coincidence that the mystics of the world's great religions are often of one mind about the need for unity, peace and the search for the Divine. [1]

Mirabai Starr [2] asserts that the God of the monotheistic faiths - Judaism, Christianity and Islam - is a 'God of Love'. We need to ask ourselves if the God we believe in is a 'God of Love' before we decide whether a passage from scriptures is helpful to our beliefs or damaging to them. As an individual who believes my faith should promote peace at every opportunity, I find the Beatitudes reassuring, but need to ask why the faith I belong to does not always uphold these values, as well as highlighting some of those instances where it does so to a very high standard.

The development of Christianity was a very complex process which is one of the reasons why there has not been an overall consensus around so fundamental an issue as peace. The ministry of Jesus and his Apostles appears to have been a peaceful one based on teaching, healing and a mendicant lifestyle, even if they were perceived by some in authority as a disruptive element due to their lack of conformity to the politics and conventions of the day. Similarly, due to their lack of temporal power, early Christian communities adapted a peaceful approach based on sharing resources for communal and charitable purposes, worshipping together and helping each other as well as resisting the states obligations to engage in pagan practices culminating in persecution and martyrdom.[3] When Christianity expanded to include non-Jews, it became a source of unity between individuals from many cultures, and multi-ethnicity has remained a feature of Christianity to this day. It spread rapidly in lands both East and West of the Roman Empire to encompass followers that were 'Coptic, Ethiopian, Celtic or Persian, for example'.[4] Christian belonging was voluntary and based on shared beliefs and practices. Krieder and Yoder [5] state that 'the church of the first three centuries was pacifist.' They cite individuals, such as Martin of Tours, who left the Roman army on their conversion to Christianity.

All this was to change after 313 A.D., when the Emperor Constantine legitimised and subsequently embraced Christianity leading to a long, messy entanglement with the powers of state. Christianity grew in popularity, power and influence within the empire and lost some of its moral authority in the process. One advantage of Christianity's new status was that it enabled a growth in the provision of charity, as service to others was a key feature of

Christian practice and the church was now able to provide hospitals, orphanages and poorhouses to assist others.[6] People often forget that Christianity originated in the East, and it continued to spread in the East, maintaining a distinctive flavour there. When these areas fell into Muslim control in subsequent years, the Eastern churches survived by adapting to their new circumstances and co-existed relatively peacefully with their Muslim neighbours for centuries. It is these communities, such as Coptic or Syrian Orthodox, that are suffering from extreme persecution in their homelands today.

When states or empires embrace a religion, that faith often gets blamed for any violence or oppression perpetrated by the political entity, although there may be different factors involved including ones that are political, historic, economic, cultural, tribal and linguistic. Sometimes the only way that individuals can distance themselves from temporal power, and its abuses, is to live a life that is countercultural. In the years after Christianity became linked to state, individuals known as the Desert Fathers and Desert Mothers escaped into the desert to try to lead a more Christ-like existence and to distance themselves from the temptations of urban life. They tried to cultivate self-awareness and wisdom and have left us with a host of sayings giving us an insight into their thinking. Many of these sayings deal with topics such as being non-judgemental and forgiving.[7] Others became 'holy fools', acting in a strange or unconventional way that went against the convention of the established church. While none of these individuals could be classified as pacifist in the modern sense of the word, they did try to avoid being caught up in temporal affairs. However, when they later banded together in monasteries, it became harder for them to avoid power, as some of their institutions earned considerable wealth and influence.

From the time of Constantine onwards, divisions between Christianity in the East and West gradually grew. The pope was based in Rome but Constantine had developed a new power base in Byzantium. Latin was prominent in the West and Greek in the East. There were theological differences between the Western and the Eastern church. The appointment of a Holy Roman Emperor in the West provided rivalry to the imperial Byzantine leadership. A formal split came with the Great Schism of 1054. This split was deepened beyond repair after Crusaders on their way to the Holy Land sacked Constantinople without provocation in 1204.[8] It is worth noting that although subsequent popes sent Crusades to the Middle East, the Eastern churches were in no way party to these enterprises and suffered greatly for them in the long run. From this point onwards, Christianity was perceived as completely split between Catholic West and Orthodox East. This fault line is very much evident today, especially in areas such as the Balkans and the Ukraine.

Catholicism brought some stability to Western Europe, but this involved a highly level of homogeneity and conformity. The 'Just War Theory' was developed by Ambrose, Augustine and Aquinas within a Catholic context and suggested that war may be morally permissible where there is a just reason for it, negotiations have failed and there is a chance of success.[9] This model still seems to hold currency with Western powers today as they continuously seek to intervene in global conflicts, but often this is just a pretext to protect their own political, economic or military interests. Although the Just War Theory does offer some scope for peacemaking efforts, it is not a pacifist standpoint. A small number of groups with pacifist leanings did emerge in Europe during the later Middle Ages, including the Waldensians in France and the Czech Brethren.[10] Some individuals also pointed towards a more peaceful and harmonious way of life. Most notable among these is St. Francis of Assisi, who rejected armed conflict, attempted to dialogue with Muslims, and who promoted love of animals and the environment. He is the patron saint of ecology. Gilbert Markus [11] reminds us that throughout the history of Christianity, many of those recognised as saints were deeply committed to seeking justice for others, individuals such as Catherine of Siena, Vincent de Paul and Thomas More.

Catholicism went more or less unchallenged in Western Europe until the Reformation when Lutheranism and Calvinism emerged. This did nothing to curb the excesses of institutional churches leading to Catholic-Protestant conflict and a new set of tyrannies including sacking of monasteries, iconoclasm, enforced puritanical practices and executions of supposed heretics. Individuals still did not have much freedom in the way they practiced their religion, with institutional Catholicism restricting Protestant practice and vica versa. The Protestant Reformation managed to spur the Catholic Church into enacting a Counter-reformation to renew its commitment to their faith. Some of the individuals who instigated reforms were mystics, like Teresa of Avila or John of the Cross in Spain, who expanded their horizons by developing links with Muslim mystics. [12] A strange hybrid emerged in England in the form of Anglicanism, which somehow managed to combine Catholic and Reformed elements within one denomination. Although not perfect, Anglicanism continues to maintain a fair degree of harmony between highly divergent theological positions, making it one of the more accommodating denominations.

For all the Reformers talk of trying to recapture the spirit of early Christianity, this did not stretch to embracing pacifism. However, the Reformation did pave the way for some more radical groups, who unlike the Lutherans, Anglicans and Calvinists, were not in any way linked to the structures of state and could, therefore, develop a more peaceful outlook. It further demonstrates that the main obstacle to Christianity embracing pacifism between the time of Constantine and the Reformation may have been the close ties that it had developed with state or empire. Once these ties were loosened or broken, opportunities were created for Christians to follow a more peaceful path.

Prior to the reformation, there were already elements of dissent and renewal within Christian Europe. Small groups, such as the already-mentioned Waldensians and Czech Brethren, developed outside the institutional church. Groups of Unitarians sprung up in Poland, Hungary and Transylvania in the mid-sixteenth century.[13] With their belief in the oneness of God, some Unitarians became interested in dialoguing with other faiths at quite an early stage, and in 1682 Unitarians sent a letter to the Moroccan ambassador in London requesting a meeting to discuss points of convergence between Unitarianism and the Muslim faith.[14] Unfortunately, this request was refused. Within the Catholic Church, individual mystics emerged such as Meister Eckhart, Hildegard of Bingen, Walter Hilton and Julian of Norwich, who, although not pacifists, were more concerned with union with the Divine and service to others than worldly conflict.[15] Groups of lay people like the Beguines and the Brothers and Sisters of the Common Life, that emerged in Northern Europe, developed a communal spirituality based on living a simple and virtuous life, rather than on cultivating the intellect.

After the Reformation groups emerged which were neither Lutheran nor Calvinist. These were known as Anabaptists, or 're-baptisers', believing in adult baptism, as only then could the person understand the full implications of it and consent to it. Some believed in looking directly to God for inspiration, rather than solely to the Bible, and they tended to live simple communal lifestyles underscored by pacifist principles. Among Anabaptist groups that have survived are the Hutterites, the Amish community of North America and the Mennonites who were followers of Menno

Simons.[16] Some of the earlier Anabaptist groups, such as some Dutch Anabaptists and the Anabaptists of Munster in Germany, embraced radicalism and were far from being pacifists. Menno Simons was the individual who did most to strengthen the Anabaptist commitment to pacifism as he travelled around Europe with his message of peace and denunciation of the more radical elements.[17] Anabaptist groups gradually became quite fossilised and legalistic before experiencing growth again in the twentieth century.[18]

Another great landmark in the history of Christian pacifism was the birth of the Quakers in seventeenth century England, amidst the turmoil of the English Civil War. George Fox, the founder, believed in the ability of individuals to be inspired by the Spirit or 'Inner Light' and that there was 'that of God in every man'.[19] Quakers, who were sometimes known as Friends or Children of Light, were, like the Anabaptists before them, severely persecuted for their beliefs.[20] Worship took place in meeting houses and consisted of silence interspersed with ministry from anyone present who felt moved by the Spirit to speak, including women, who held equal status.[21] The Quaker commitment to pacifism became evident quite early in their development and was encapsulated in the Peace Testimony of the 'Harmless and Innocent People of God, called Quakers' addressed to King Charles the Second in 1660.[22]

It is worth quoting part here:

'We utterly deny all outward wars and strife, and fighting with outward weapons, for any end, or under any pretence whatever; this is our testimony to the whole world. The Spirit of Christ by which we are guided is not changeable, so as once to command us from a thing as evil and again to move unto it; we certainly know and testify to the world, that the spirit of Christ, which leads us to all Truth, will never move us to fight and war against any man with

7

outward weapons, neither for the kingdom of Christ nor for the kingdoms of the world'.[23]

It is interesting to note in the above statement, that it clarifies Quakers were unwilling to take up arms for either religious or political reasons i.e. 'neither for the kingdom of God nor the kingdoms of the world'. This should have been enough to allay fears that Quakers were a threat to any particular interests but, despite this reassurance, persecutions continued. It sometimes appears that people often feel as threatened by pacifism as they do by aggression. Quakers went on to uphold their Peace Testimony attempting to treat the Native Americans fairly as well as leading the way in the campaign to abolish slavery. They managed to continue to live a peaceful way of life by adhering to the basic principles of peace, truth, simplicity and equality, values which were mutually-reinforcing. Quakers were joined in their fight against slavery by other Christians, such as the Anglican evangelical William Wilberforce.[24]

In the nineteenth and early twentieth century, with growth of empires and improved communication and transport, people came into contact with others more than in the past, leading to the development of new and cross-fertilisation of older religious, social and political ideas. Although not a Christian, an Indian, Rammohun Roy, under the influence of Unitarian ideas, encouraged joint worship between Christians and Hindus and wrote a book called 'The Precepts of Jesus – The Guide to Peace and Happiness'.[25] Later in the nineteenth century, Unitarians such as Ralph Waldo Emerson, promoted the Transcendentalist view that religious truth could be discerned through intuition and nature.[26] This paved the way for others, such as Thoreau, to pursue a simpler, more ecological and peaceful way of life. Emerson also introduced a number of Hindu concepts into his thinking, further increasing the interest in other religions among Unitarians. In 1894, Tolstoy wrote an impassioned plea for the adoption of Christian pacifism, entitled 'The Kingdom of God is within You', in which he cites international influences on his thinking, such as the Quakers. Sharma [27] describes how Gandhi first came to understand, respect and be influenced by Christians when he came to 'pluralist London'. Inter-religious dialogue started in earnest with the World Parliament of Religions in Chicago in 1893, and other gatherings in subsequent years that brought people from different faiths together.[28] Paramahansa Yogananda describes how he was asked to address an International Congress of Religious Liberals in Boston in 1920.[29] There he met individuals from free-thinking groups, such as the Unitarians. Similarly, when writer and painter Khalil Gibran moved from his native Lebanon to the United States in the early twentieth century, he was exposed to a number of social and religious influences that helped shape his work and led him to believe that 'unity is the essential truth of religion'.[30]

Much of the development in Christian pacifism and peacemaking in the twentieth century occurred in reaction to external events such as international and global conflicts. These included the Boer War, World War One and Two, the advent of chemical weapons, the dropping of nuclear bombs on Hiroshima and Nagasaki, the Partition of India, the Cold War, the Korean War, the Vietnam War, numerous civil wars and the seemingly endless conflict in the Middle East. Some of these events created new circumstances that demanded creative and humane responses. Peace churches, such as the Quakers and Mennonites, continued to uphold their pacifist principles but now mainstream churches also began to develop approaches that were more peaceful, and some individuals within those denominations chose to adopt a more pacifist approach to their faith.

In a way, the coming of modernity may have made it easier for Christians and churches to embrace peace work. Increased

9

secularisation in the West helped highlight some of the real causes of conflict. Unfortunately, there is much evidence of Church complicity with tyranny. Examples include Catholic support for the fascist Ustashe party in wartime Croatia and for the dictator Franco in Spain and evangelical backing of U.S. militarism. There are many people who blame religion for all the ills of the world, ignoring other factors. It is difficult for the Christian pacifist to counter these accusations, without going on the counter-offensive, and leaving themselves open to charges of aggression. It is difficult for the secularist and the religious adherent to see eye-to-eye, due to their sometimes widely-differing worldviews. Yet, much of the criticism levelled at religious adherents by secular critics may be inaccurate and unfair. Some secularists think it is easy to write the religious adherent off as 'feeble-minded' or 'bad-minded' and to catalogue all the ills that they are responsible for. They accuse religious people of being anti-science when they question the ethics behind certain practices. They are sometimes simultaneously accused of being both anti-science and responsible for environmental damage, which may be a bit of a contradiction.

Critics, such as Richard Dawkins, should be asking why a huge percentage of his fellow scientists are working anonymously for the military, greedy corporations and rogue governments, engaged in activities such as developing high-tech, chemical and nuclear weapons, experimenting on animals, poisoning our food chain and destroying the environment. Kent [31] quotes Pope John Paul the Second, in a message to the Pontifical Academy of Sciences in 1983, saying: 'When, in a particular historical situation, it is all but inevitable that a certain form of scientific research will be used for purposes of aggression, the scientist must make a choice that will enable him to work for the good of the people, for the building up of peace. By refusing certain fields of research, inevitably destined, in the concrete historical circumstances, for deadly purposes, the scientists of the whole world ought to be united in a common readiness to disarm science and to form a providential force for peace.' This is not being anti-science; it is being pro-humanity and is commendable.

Churches do not have as much political influence today as in the past. Many politicians, scientists, bankers, corporation CEO's, military leaders may have more of a role in creating conflict than your average church leader. After all, the Vatican, that international symbol of ecclesiastical power, has a budget which is only a tiny fraction of what the UK spends on its nuclear arsenal. The vicious bands of Muslim fanatics currently terrorising areas of the Middle East only emerged after secularist Western powers blew a hole in civilisation there, creating a power vacuum for anyone to step into. The Serbian Orthodox Church received much blame for the conflict in former Yugoslavia after former Communist politicians co-opted the symbols of Orthodoxy in their fight to gain control of the area. Although, some of the clergy were happy to go along with this, only 5% of the Serb population were thought to have any links with the church at this time, after decades of Communist rule. In Ireland, during 'The Troubles', it tended to be Marxist ideologues rather than clergy, who supported the IRA. At Easter 2016, the centenary of the 1916 Easter Rising was being 'celebrated' by government and media, rather than being commemorated in any spiritually meaningful way. Sometimes, the political, religious, economic and cultural are intertwined in the most intricate and confusing way.

Although the churches may not be directly responsible for war and violence, given their spiritual remit, they could sometimes do more to counteract conflict and to actively promote peace. This does not mean being disloyal to nations, withholding chaplaincy services or denying fallen combatants a Christian burial. But churches could be more critical of governments that bomb foreign territories or who

11

recruit vulnerable young people to the army because they know that if they tried to recruit them when they were older they would refuse. Maybe, churches should consider being more frequently critical of the possession of nuclear weapons and more supportive of conscientious objectors. They should teach the message of peace in an uncompromising way, and while acknowledging that war and conflict may be a fact of life, this does not mean the Christian message should be used to justify it.

The developments in Christian pacifism and peacemaking since the start of the twentieth century are too complex to be presented as a unified process in a short overview such as this, but the following are some events worthy of note. In 1899, Gandhi organised an Indian Ambulance Corps within the British forces at the start of the Boer War in South Africa.[32] He was criticised for this action and accused of supporting British aggression. Whatever the ethics of the situation, Gandhi wanted to show that he was loyal to the British Empire but that he did not approve of taking up arms and this was his response to the situation. This provided a precedent for the foundation of the Friends Ambulance Unit during World War One. Gandhi may be the single most influential figure in the history of non-violence in the twentieth century. Many notable Christian pacifists, including Martin Luther King, credited him with influencing their actions. Gandhi himself was greatly influenced by the Russian writer and Christian pacifist Leo Tolstoy, and he attributes his conversion to non-violence to reading Tolstoy's 'The Kingdom of God is within You'.[33] Gandhi also embraced Tolstoy's belief that the number of British in India was so minute in relation to the Indian population, that they could easily be overthrown through peaceful resistance.

Quakers founded many Peace Societies at the beginning of the twentieth century and the National Peace Council came into being in 1908.[34] An international dimension was also being added to peace work, with Peace Conferences held in major European cities annually prior to the First World War and a Court of International Justice being set up in the Hague in 1907.[35] Unfortunately, these initiatives were not enough to avert large scale armed conflict in 1914. Among the responses of Quakers to the First World War, were to set up the Friends Ambulance Unit and a War Victims Relief Committee which oversaw work with refugees and dispossessed in Britain, France, Russia and elsewhere.[36] After the introduction of the Conscription Act in 1916, many conscientious objectors were imprisoned for refusing to fight.

The advent of war on such a global scale brought about a dramatic change in perspective in many individual Christian believers. Alexander [37] states that a Cambridge conference of Christian pacifists, which led to the formation of the Fellowship of Reconciliation, was such 'a significant sign of the development of the Christian conscience in relation to war that, by 1914, there were many men and women in all the main Christian denominations of England who were convinced that all war, even a 'righteous' war of defence, was impossible for the Christian, and that he must give himself completely, in war-time as in times of peace, to the ministry of reconciliation.' Krieder and Yoder [38] point out how liberal Christian pacifists, many of whom placed their trust in the newly-formed League of Nations, had their illusions shattered by the rise to power of Hitler in the 1930's and the ensuing destruction of the Second World War.

With the Second World War, there arose a whole new set of ethical issues, such as the spread of modern warfare globally, the arial bombardment of cities and civilian areas, the genocide of Jews and mass murder of gypsies, disabled and gay people, the creation of massive numbers of refugees and perhaps the most unforeseen, the dropping of atomic bombs on the Japanese cities of Hiroshima and

Nagasaki. Despite the best efforts of Gandhi, which led to his assassination, India was partitioned into two separate states, India and Pakistan, on gaining its independence from British rule. This was followed by bloody massacres and the mass movement of Muslims from India to Pakistan and Hindus and Sikhs from Pakistan to India. The foundation of the State of Israel in 1948 led to war and discord in the Middle East. Many Americans lost their lives in combat in Korea in the 1950's. By the time of the Vietnam war in the 1960's, not everyone was keen to go and fight, leading to the formation of a mass anti-war movement in which many Christian peace activists were involved. Also, in the US in the 1960's, a mass civil rights movement arose, protesting peacefully against the unjust discrimination against Blacks in society. Its leader, Martin Luther King, a Baptist minister influenced by Gandhian methods of non-violent action, was, just like Gandhi, assassinated. The so-called Cold War, a mutually aggressive military stand-off between 'Communist East' and 'Capitalist West', greatly heightened fear of nuclear war, leading to large scale anti-nuclear movements and protests, especially in Europe. Campaign for Nuclear Disarmament (CND) rallies in Britain managed to mobilise large numbers of the young, and not so young, and there was also a specifically Christian branch of this organisation. Interest in challenging nuclear arsenals abated with the demise of Communism and the end of the Cold War.

However, new concerns replaced old ones. The brutal civil war in former Yugoslavia reminded Europeans that their continent was still not immune to serious conflict. The religious dimension to this war was disturbing but needs to be understood and assessed in the context of a long and complex history in which the religions involved co-existed for centuries under various regimes. In some cities, such as Sarajevo, Orthodox and Catholic churches, along with mosques and synagogues could be found, side by side, within small areas, reflecting a long record of multi-faith co-existence not seen in comparable cities in Western Europe. This diversity became a weak point after the fall of the Communist regime and former Communist politicians latched on to religious symbolism in order to seize power in particular enclaves setting neighbour against neighbour. The role of propaganda in these types of conflicts is paramount in order to make individuals begin to suspect and fear people they have lived and worked with all their lives. Conflict thrives in areas where there is a power vacuum and similar circumstances have been created in the Middle East after decades of disputes aggravated by interference by outside powers seeking to maintain political, economic and military influence. Christians, such as Archbishop Desmond Tutu, were instrumental in bringing down the apartheid system in South Africa and implementing the Truth and Reconciliation process to try and create a peaceful transition to democracy there.

After the fall of Communism, battle lines were redrawn between the secular, highly individualistic and capitalist West and the Muslim world, resulting in the Gulf War, the attack on and destruction of the World Trade Centre and the ensuing invasions of Afghanistan and Iraq by Britain and the US followed more recently by the destabilisation of and civil war in Syria. The power vacuum in large parts of the Middle East has left minorities there open to brutal oppression by extremist elements. The two thousand year-old Christian community is being persecuted almost to extinction. Although ordinary Muslims are not to blame for this, more extreme Islamic elements accuse the Middle Eastern Christians of being lackeys of the West. Nothing could be further from the truth. The Middle Eastern churches existed prior to any European church and pre-date the Muslim community by hundreds of years. They worship in ancient languages such as Coptic and Syriac. Although the first major source of conflict between the West and East was the Crusades, these were waged by the Western Church and the Middle Eastern churches were not involved. Again today, the Middle Eastern churches are paying the price for Western aggression, this time by secular governments, and the secular citizens of those Western nations are immune to the sufferings of these ancient communities. The new forms of high tech warfare employed by Western governments, such as the use of drones to assassinate opponents, means that they can interfere militarily in weaker countries without sustaining huge casualties that would make them unpopular at home. They can wage military campaigns, and even destroy a country's infrastructure, without creating any sense at home of being a nation at war. Warfare is now often covert and sinister with citizens of Western countries having little knowledge of and still less say over conflicts waged in their name. Even though they show concern for the hordes of refugees created by conflict, there is a reluctance to take the steps necessary to relieve their plight. Churches overall have a good record of championing the cause of refugees, as well as helping in real terms, as the notion of hospitality is central to all the major religions. Unfortunately, there are some traditionalist church people who buck this trend and advocate closing borders to those without the means to support themselves. Meanwhile, many Muslims in Europe and North America are treated with suspicion and regarded as terrorists or potential terrorists. The sources of this hatred include both right-wing Christians and a new breed of secularist who believes that their right to free speech includes the right to denigrate others due to their religious beliefs. For instance, North African Muslims have suffered decades of discrimination from the French government and deserve better than to have their beliefs mocked or demonised by a secularist media who then do nothing to accept responsibility for fuelling violence. Where does violence begin, if not with lack of understanding compounded through verbal abuse. Therefore, it is important that Christians always speak respectfully about others even if they have genuine criticisms of them.

We have seen that the twentieth and early twenty first centuries have presented Christians and other religious people with many new challenges in terms of promoting a peaceful world. These challenges include large scale warfare, high tech weapons, increased propaganda, chemical weapons, nuclear weapons, genocide, refugees and displaced persons, environmental damage, Post-traumatic Stress Disorder (PTSD), water shortages, increased materialism, etc. The novelty of some of these challenges demanded responses that were creative and effective and luckily some of these responses were forthcoming. They include conscientious objection, the formation of justice and peace groups, the awarding of peace prizes, the founding of international bodies such as NGO'S and the United Nations, contributions from dedicated peaceful individuals, anti-war marches, providing sanctuary to refugees, inter-faith dialogue, non-violent action, creating peace gardens, educating others about peace, campaigning and lobbying, creating art and literature that promotes a peaceful message, creating sacred spaces, implementing restorative justice and truth commissions, etc. Christians and other religious individuals should try to ensure that their actions are always peaceful and not motivated by other factors disguised as a desire for peace. For instance, sometimes individuals attend anti-war marches because of hatred for their government rather than a genuine desire for peace. The words they write on their placards and the slogans they chant or the fierce look in their eyes betrays their motives. This should not be the approach of the Christian, who should be motivated by love and compassion for their fellow humans, although, they may sometimes be forced to use harsh words. The approach to peace by the Christian pacifist or peacemaker should be subtly different from that of the protester motivated purely by political ideals. For instance, the Christian peacemaker may opt for a silent vigil, rather than a slogan-filled march, if uncomfortable with some of the sentiments expressed. The next section will look in detail at some of the responses that Christians have offered in response to conflict.

2. Methods:

It is one thing to hold pacifist principles, but quite another to be able to find ways to enlist these principles in the promotion of peace. Christian pacifists and peacemakers throughout the ages have reacted in different ways to the challenges they were faced with and come up with varied strategies to live out their principles. This section will look at some of the peaceful initiatives taken by Christians to promote peace. Some of the people mentioned in this section will be profiled in greater detail later in the book.

Some Christians, such as the early Christians, and later the Anabaptists, chose to live relatively self-contained lives, and were not dependent on a civil society that did not share their ideals. To an extent, the Amish of North America still adopt this strategy, living in tightly-knit communities that reject modernity and use horse-drawn buggies rather than cars, for example. Gasgoigne [1] points out the irony of people living a traditional lifestyle like this, being up-to-date in being environment-friendly. However, it is not necessary to go to such lengths to live a simple life, and many Christians try to do this without disengaging from the wider society they live in. Many Quakers have managed to do this in a balanced way.

Groups such as the Mennonites and Quakers also have a long tradition of abstaining from military service. Alexander [2] states that although the 1916 Conscription Act in Britain made provision for conscientious objection, it was so badly administered that many conscientious objectors, including Quakers, ended up in prison. If they refused to join the armed services on their release from prison, they were sentenced all over again. Christians from other denominations often became conscientious objectors too, such as the

Austrian Catholic layman, Franz Jaggerstatter, who paid with his life during the Second World War for refusing to fight for the Germans.[3]

To counteract the accusation that conscientious objectors are disloyal or lacking in courage because they refuse to fight, some Christian individuals and groups, such as Quakers, 'have built a reputation for war relief work, reconstruction and conflict transformation'.[4] A Swiss Quaker, Pierre Ceresole, was instrumental, through the Service Civil International and the International Voluntary Service for Peace, in setting up work camps where pacifists could demonstrate their willingness to contribute to society.[5] Although Catholic monk and 1960's peace advocate Thomas Merton believed that Christians should renounce violence, he also thought it was important to actively oppose oppression, and was drawn to the active non-violence lived by Gandhi and Dorothy Day.[6] Gandhi, and later Martin Luther King, demonstrated that it was possible to stand up to oppressive forces without resorting to violence. One major concern that Merton had regarding mass peace movements was that they lacked compassion and were often motivated by rage towards those they perceived as perpetrating injustices; without compassion, Merton believed, individuals could not become genuine agents for change.[7] One alternative to a noisy protest, often used by some to promote political interests that are not directly related to peace, may be to participate in a peace vigil, which negates the opportunities for noisy sloganeering. While the role he played in the peace movement was restricted, due to being a Trappist monk, Thomas Merton used his correspondence with others to promote peace. Letter writing can be a powerful tool to promote peace and human rights. We saw earlier how George Fox wrote to King Charles the Second informing him of the Quaker Peace Testimony. People often write to their MP to highlight various injustices. Amnesty International, founded by Catholic Peter Beneson, encouraged letter writing to promote Human Rights and to champion the rights of prisoners. Now people also use more up-to-date methods such as e-mails and blogs to get their message across. The use of social media is becoming more central to organising peaceful resistance to tyranny in countries where it is too dangerous for groups to gather. Thomas Merton also used his art and writing to promote the way of peace. Art and literature can be a creative, subtle and rewarding way to highlight peace and justice issues.

Providing hospitality and sanctuary has always been part of the Christian tradition and that of other religions. Individual churches and Christian agencies have a record of providing help and relief to refugees and for campaigning on their behalf e.g. the Jesuit Refugee Service. Coupled with this, is the use of sacred space to promote peaceful co-existence. Coventry Cathedral was very badly damaged by bombing during the Blitz, when Coventry itself was nearly levelled. Instead of rebuilding it in a conventional way after the war, the damaged part was left the way it was as a reminder of what had occurred, and a modern part was added on for worship, so that the whole building could be a memorial to peace. A bombed-out church in central Liverpool was also left in its damaged state as a memorial. St. Ethelburga's Church, in the City of London, damaged by an IRA bomb in 1993, is now used as a centre for Reconciliation and Peace.

Another positive way to help create peace, unity and harmony is inter-religious or interfaith dialogue. Interfaith dialogue, of sorts, goes back a long way. Francis of Assisi dialogued with Muslims in the Holy Land. Medieval Christian mystic Raymond Lull is supposed to have met with North African Sufis (Cato: 1994: p40-42).[8] Spanish Counter-reformation mystic, John of the Cross, is likewise said to have sought out these Muslim holy men and poets. The Jesuits sought dialogue with the Asian elites, not just on religious topics, but scientific subjects too.[9] While much of this was done in a triumphalist spirit, often with a view to making conversions, the protagonists often learned from each other, or at least learned to respect each other and their respective beliefs. As we saw previously, early Unitarians sought to initiate dialogue with Muslims in the seventeenth century and Hindus in the nineteenth century. Religions began to come together in more democratic ways from the time of the first World Parliament of Religions in 1893. In the twentieth century, two separate strands of dialogue came to the forefront; ecumenism which sought to promote understanding and unity between different Christian denominations, and interfaith dialogue which sought to heal divisions between different religious traditions. The World Council of Churches, founded in Geneva in 1948, and receiving much support from Protestant and Orthodox churches, led the way in promoting ecumenism.[10] Ecumenism is not as strong as it was previously, due to the further fragmentation of Christianity with the growth of Pentecostal, Charismatic and Evangelical churches, which promote a very individualist style of faith, sometimes not much interested in forging links with others. However, there are signs that this situation may be changing, with Pentecostal pastors getting involved in peace and human rights issues in places like Zimbabwe. Since Vatican Two, the Roman Catholic church has become more interested in dialoguing with other denominations and other faiths than before. In 1986, Pope John Paul the Second, convened a meeting of religious leaders from all the main traditions in Assisi, the birthplace of St. Francis, for a World Day of Prayer for Peace. More recently, Pope Francis has extended the hand of peace to many, whether Christian, secular or belonging to other religious traditions. In 2016 he published an influential encyclical letter on the environment entitled Laudata Si'. Catholic organisations have become prominent in recent decades promoting peace, justice and development, examples being Pax Christi, Caritas and the Sant' Egidio Community. Local Catholic diocese's also have their own Justice and Peace groups.

The awarding of peace prizes, though it may seem like a vain process, helps highlight the work of dedicated individuals committed to pursuing various peace causes, and where there is a monetary component to the prize, the money may be used to finance the cause further. The most famous and prominent of these prizes is the Nobel Peace Prize, which was established in 1901, and is both highly regarded and sometimes controversial. Among Christians in receipt of this award are Albert Schweitzer, Dominique Pire, Dag Hammarskjold, Martin Luther King, Mother Teresa, Desmond Tutu, John Hume, Jimmy Carter and the Quakers. Some Christian organisations, such as Pax Christi International, award their own peace prizes. Recipients have included the Jesuit Refugee Service and Franjo Starcevic, a Croatian pacifist. The prizes may serve to highlight causes and provide hope and incentive to those involved with them as peace work can drag on for long periods of time with little evident progress.

Promoting restorative justice, through Truth and Reconciliation Commissions such as that held in South Africa under the leadership of Archbishop Desmond Tutu, may also be an area where Christians, with their emphasis on the importance of truth and forgiveness, may be able to make a valuable contribution. The Catholic Sant' Egidio Community has played a leading role as a trusted mediator in conflicts such as those in Mozambique and the Balkans and has been awarded many prestigious peace accolades for this work.

We have seen how Christians in the past have responded to the call of peace in a number of different ways, some based on dissent, others on creativity and dialogue. Many of these initiatives would not have happened but for the drive and sacrifice of committed individuals. To some, pacifism and non-violence may seem ineffectual and like a soft option. However, it is worth remembering that while in a democracy it can require drastic actions to get noticed, for those living under tyranny even a critical word can land individuals in prison or worse.

3. People:

This section will profile individual Christians who are / were either pacifists or committed to peacemaking. Some of these individuals became peacemakers due to the pressure of their own circumstances, such as Martin Luther King who grew up in the deeply segregated society of the Southern United States. Others, like Archbishop Romero, became peacemakers reluctantly, after being forced to acknowledge the injustices of the society around them. Some individuals made a commitment to peacemaking voluntarily through becoming aware of the plight of others. Jesuit priest and peacemaker John Dear describes how he became committed to the path of peace after a transformative pilgrimage to the Holy Land in 1982 just before joining his order. What he thought was going to be a restful trip turned out to be an education in the conflict of the region.[1] Others may not have viewed themselves as peacemakers, never mind pacifists, but still were honoured for their contribution to peace because of their work. Mother Teresa, who would probably have perceived herself more as a servant to the poor than a peacemaker, was none-the-less awarded the Nobel Peace Prize in 1979, as her tackling of poverty was seen as a contribution to a more harmonious world. The Christian pacifists and peacemakers profiled in this section represent a great variety of causes, perspectives and approaches. Some, such as Desmond Tutu, have a high global profile, whereas others, such as Bruce Kent, may only really be recognisable locally or nationally. The individuals featured below are only a sample of those who could have been included but comprise a cross-section that is representative of nationality, denomination and period. Details of some useful and relevant websites, articles and books have been included at the end of the profiles.

Karen Armstrong (1944-): Karen Armstrong is a renowned and respected writer on religious themes, especially the history of religion and interfaith issues. She started her working life as a novice nun in a Catholic convent but left because of the unreasonableness of some of the things that were expected of her in order to conform to a vow of obedience .[2] She recorded these experiences in a book entitled 'Through the Narrow Gate'. She gave up on the idea of being a full-time academic after an unsuccessful attempt to gain a master's degree in English. This does not seem to have worked against her, as she went on to develop a highly successful career as a freelance writer and broadcaster. She wrote widely on the development of the main faiths in books such as 'The History of God' (1993) and 'The Great Transformation' (2006). She was instrumental in drawing up the Charter for Compassion, intended to strengthen ethical priorities across the religions and signed by the Dalai Lama, Queen Noor of Jordan and Desmond Tutu, among others. She is highly regarded for her objectivity and has received a number of awards and honorary degrees.

• See www.charterforcompassion.org for further information.

Joan Baez (1941-): Baez is an American folk singer and peace activist who came to prominence in the 1960's when she was best known for her protest songs. Her father was Mexican and her family converted to Quakerism, two factors which may have directed her focus towards peace and justice issues early on in life. Due to her father's work, she lived in a number of different countries while growing up including Spain, Canada, England, France and the Middle East. Her musical career was greatly influenced by Pete Seeger, also a protest singer. Her close association with Bob Dylan may have contributed to her renown, but it was in fact she who introduced Dylan into the folk scene. As well as being an accomplished singer and musician, she has throughout her career been committed to a wide range of peace and justice issues. These include participating in the Civil Rights Movement, opposing the Vietnam War, advocating human rights through Amnesty International, campaigning against the death penalty and promoting environmental causes, along with a whole range of other issues. In recognition of this work and commitment, Amnesty International inaugurated the Amnesty International Joan Baez Award, to be awarded to artists, writers or musicians who make an outstanding contribution to human rights. In 1975, Baez won the Thomas Merton Award for her contribution to peace.

- See www.joanbaez.com for further information.

Bartholomew 1 of Constantinople – Ecumenical Patriarch (1940-): Bartholomew is the highly respected spiritual leader of the Eastern Orthodox world. His influence over the autocephalous, or independent, churches of Eastern Orthodoxy has more to do with respect and persuasion rather than any direct temporal power. His efforts to promote interfaith relations, human rights and care for the environment has earned him the nickname of the 'Green Patriarch'. He is a keen advocate of interfaith dialogue and he has built up a good rapport with Pope Francis and maintains contacts with prominent Jews and Muslims. He is an advocate of religious freedom and is well aware of the importance of this due to persecution of the Orthodox community by the Turkish authorities in Istanbul where he is based. He was instrumental in arranging the Pan-Orthodox Council in Crete in 2016. The importance of this Council, which was the first of its kind in 1200 years, cannot be overstated and was vital to the promotion of Orthodox unity. Unfortunately, there is also much resentment in the Orthodox world of his influence and the Russian Orthodox Church, along with four other churches, chose to boycott the event. The Russian Church, which represents the greatest percentage of Orthodox believers, states that this invalidates the

Council's claim to be representative.[3] He has endeavoured to improve relations between his church and Catholics and travelled to Lesbos with Pope Francis in an attempt to highlight the plight of Middle Eastern refugees there. He has been awarded a number of prizes including the Congressional Gold Medal from the U.S. Government, the Sophie Prize (for environmental work) and the Order of the Star of Romania along with numerous doctorates from universities around the world.

- See www.patriarchate.org for further information.

Bishop George Bell (1883-1958): George Bell was the Bishop of Chichester from the late 1920's to the late 1950's. He was ordained after studying in Oxford and served as a 'slum priest' in Leeds. During the First World War, he was appointed to undertake inter-denominational work and also engaged in work to help war orphans and to promote the exchange of prisoners of war. While Dean of Canterbury in the 1920's, he received Gandhi at the cathedral. Through his inter-denominational work, he had close ties with the Lutheran church in Germany. He strongly opposed the accommodations made with the Nazi's by the German Evangelical Church and was supportive of the Confessing Church which opposed Nazi policies. He was friends with Dietrich Bonhoeffer, who was later executed for plotting against Hitler, and who passed on to Bell information about what was really happening in Germany and about the rise of anti-Semitism. Bell then publicised this information through the press. He signed the Barmen Declaration which expressed the Confessing Church's opposition to Nazi interference in church affairs. He worked hard on behalf of refugees fleeing Germany. After the war started he advocated for both conscientious objectors and German prisoners of war. He gained notoriety for his condemnation of intensive bombing by either side of cities and civilian areas. Although a life-long peacemaker, he was not a pacifist and supported the German resistance. After the war, he drew attention to, and protested against, the expulsion of millions of Germans from surrounding central and east European countries. He was also a firm opponent of nuclear weapons. Bell died in 1958, but his reputation has been marred in recent years through allegations of historical sexual abuse. Many have come to his defence, saying that as these are only allegations and he is not alive to defend himself, this information should not be used to destroy his reputation.

- See www.georgebellgroup.org for further information.

Daniel Berrigan (1921-2016): Fr. Daniel Berrigan was an American Jesuit priest, poet, university lecturer and peace activist. After his ordination in 1952, Berrigan worked to tackle poverty. He became more radicalised after contact with French Jesuits in the early nineteen-sixties and founded the Catholic Peace Fellowship with his brother Philip and began to actively oppose the Vietnamese War. He continued with his university teaching and writing poetry throughout this period. He became more committed to non-violent actions after his brother was imprisoned for six years for his part in anti-war protests. He advocated for improvements for prisoners of war and made a visit to Vietnam in 1968 to see for himself the situation there. His actions, although remaining non-violent, became more provocative to the authorities and in 1968 Berrigan and his brother Philip and seven other Catholic protesters burned hundreds of draft files with homemade napalm in Catonsville Maryland. After an initial period on the run and on the FBI's 'most wanted' list, Berrigan was eventually arrested and sentenced to three year's imprisonment. Non-violent acts of civil disobedience such as these helped shape a new direction in the approach of the anti-war movement. Later in his career, Berrigan campaigned against nuclear proliferation through the Plowshares Movement, founded by Berrigan, his brother and other activists. Actions included attempts to damage nuclear warheads and the pouring of blood on related documents. Berrigan continued to protest against later US military offensives, such as those in Iraq and Kosovo. The Berrigan brothers engaged in the tough end of non-violent acts of civil disobedience, not for everyone and definitely not for the faint-hearted. The peace movement requires people with different natures, abilities and perspectives to work together and to make the best of what they have to offer. Whereas Daniel Berrigan was determined enough, committed enough and tough enough to carry out high profile non-violent acts, others contributed in other ways. An example of this was the Trappist monk Thomas Merton, a friend of the Berrigan's, who supported the peace movement pastorally through his letters and who occasionally offered a critical voice, such as when he cautioned against the peace movement being fuelled by negative emotions such as anger and rage and advocated that it needed more compassion.[4] This is a good example of action being supported by prayer, contemplation and wisdom.

- See Reed, C in The Guardian: 02/05/2016 (www.theguardian.com) for more information.

Philip Berrigan (1923-2002): Philip Berrigan was an ex-Catholic priest and an American peace activist. His pacifism was shaped by his experiences of active service during the Second World War. In the nineteen-fifties he was ordained a Josephite priest and also began to teach at university level. He was jailed in the early nineteen-sixties for his role in the Civil Rights Movement and his actions began to meet with disapproval within his religious order. Along with his Jesuit brother Daniel, he got more deeply involved with the anti-war movement. Along with three other activists, he symbolically poured blood over draft records in Baltimore, earning Berrigan a six-year sentence in a federal prison. After an early release, he and his brother, along with other activists, were sentenced to three years each for burning draft records in Catonsville, Maryland. Berrigan engaged in similar actions until the end of the Vietnamese War in 1975. The participants in these protests needed to be committed to non-violence and be prepared to face the ensuing consequences for their actions. They were often members of Catholic religious orders and went on retreats beforehand to discern their commitment. After leaving the priesthood, Berrigan married an ex-nun Elizabeth MacAlister and together they founded Jonah House in Baltimore, which serves as a base for the Plowshares Movement, set up by the Berrigan brothers to oppose nuclear weapons. By the time of his death in 2002, Berrigan had been jailed repeatedly for his convictions and Jonah House continues to be run by his widow. Mirabai Starr [5] writes with great affection of the hospitality she received from Elizabeth MacAlister, and other activists, while staying there. She said they consoled her because she felt guilty working as an academic, and writing about religion, while they were out living it through non-violent actions. They told her that she was contributing by providing access to spiritual writings that can serve as an inspiration to those trying to live out their faith.

- See www.jonahhouse.org for further information.

Vera Brittain (1893-1970): Vera Brittain was a writer and pacifist who saw first-hand the devastating effects of war while serving as a nurse during the First World War, first in England and later at the front in France where she was involved in nursing German casualties. She recorded these experiences, which moulded her pacifism, in her autobiographical Testament of Youth published in the nineteen thirties. As well as witnessing and experiencing the effects of war, she also lost some of those dearest to her in this conflict including her brother, Martin, her fiancé, Roland, and friends Victor and Geoffrey. She joined the Anglican Pacifist Fellowship in the late nineteen thirties under the influence of Dick Sheppard.

29

Though a pacifist, Brittain contributed to the war effort during World War Two through working as a fire warden. Kent [6] states that he admires Brittain because she never gave up and responded to the mistakes repeated by governments with integrity, through writing a monthly newsletter to pacifist friends, in condemning blanket-bombing of German cities and after the war through providing relief to impoverished German civilians. Brittain was a regular contributer to Peace News, founded by Quaker Humphrey Moore, and also campaigned against nuclear weapons.

- See www.ppu.org.uk for further information.

Jimmy Carter (1924-2015): Jimmy Carter was President of the USA between 1977 and 1981. He was awarded the Nobel Peace Prize in 2002, more for his achievements after he left office than his presidential work. Carter came from the southern U.S. state of Georgia and was raised a Baptist. His naval career lasted from the Second World War right up till the 1950's. He then went into farming for a number of years before embarking on his political career. On becoming President, Carter pardoned all conscientious objectors from the Vietnam War. He role was central in the Camp David Accords between Israel and Egypt in 1978. In 1982, he set up the Carter Centre to promote human rights. He was also involved in the Christian housing charity Habitat for Humanity which seeks to address housing problems globally and took part in housebuilding projects on their behalf. The Carter Centre promotes democracy, fair elections, public health, human rights and peace work worldwide. Carter was awarded the Nobel Peace Prize in recognition of this work. He was active in promoting peace in diverse areas such as north Korea, Vietnam, Africa, the Middle East and Latin America as well as opposing the death penalty and torture. He also wrote prolifically on a number of topics including peace and human rights.

- See www.cartercenter.org for further information.

Pierre Ceresole (1879-1945): Ceresole was a Swiss Quaker who believed that it was necessary for conscientious objectors to come up with a way to demonstrate that they were not averse to work or to contributing to society even if they were not prepared to join the armed forces. The solution he came up with was to organise work camps during the summer, where international groups of pacifists could come together to do relief work, becoming known as the International Voluntary Service for Peace (IVSP).[7] His wife decided to publish his personal and inspiring journals after his death.

- See Durham: 2010 for further information.

Dorothy Day (1897-1980): Dorothy Day was born in New York and raised in the Episcopalian Church. After leaving college, she worked as a journalist and was involved in left-wing politics. When she had a child in 1926, she had it baptised Catholic and converted herself shortly afterwards. She felt unsupported as a single mother by the Church and struggled reconciling her faith to her commitment to social justice. With encouragement from the Catholic philosopher and activist Peter Maurin, she set up the Catholic Worker newspaper to promote a radical interpretation of the Gospels that favoured the poor and powerless. She also set up a house of hospitality to provide food and shelter for the homeless. As well as setting up houses of hospitality, she became committed to the cause of non-violence, which she believed was integral to the Sermon on the Mount. She maintained this position throughout the Second World War and the ensuing Cold War. Her uniqueness lay in her deep dedication to prayer, service to the poor and pacifism, simultaneously.[8]

- See www.catholicworker.org for further information.

John Dear (1959-): Dear joined the Jesuits in 1982. Prior to entering this order, he went on a pilgrimage to the Holy Land which he claims opened his eyes to peace and justice issues.[9] Dear has been arrested several times and been imprisoned for non-violent acts of civil disobedience such as breaking into air force bases and damaging warplanes. He has turned his hand to many roles including teaching theology, serving as a pastor, working for the Jesuit Refugee Service in El Salvador, co-ordinating chaplaincy services in New York after September 11th, 2001, serving as Director for the Fellowship of Reconciliation and addressing churches and other organisations on peace issues. One theme that constantly emerges when writing about those who work in this area is how threatening many people seem to find any talk of peace, almost like a declaration of war. Dear [10] describes the hostility and verbal abuse he sometimes experiences when he speaks to church audiences about the folly and immorality of war. He has led interfaith groups to the Middle East and set up a Pax Christi regional group in New Mexico. He has written several books on peace and non-violence and been nominated for the Nobel Peace Prize on numerous occasions, including a nomination by Desmond Tutu. He left the Jesuit Order in 2013 following a disagreement about approaches to peace and justice.

- See www.fatherjohndear.org for further information.

Jim Forest (1941 -): Forest converted to Catholicism while in the U.S. Navy and was discharged as a conscientious objector. He became involved with various peace groups in the 1960's including the Catholic Worker, Catholic Peace Fellowship and the Fellowship of Reconciliation. He was imprisoned along with thirteen others, some of them priests, for breaking into draft board offices and destroying files after at a prayer meeting. He accompanied the Buddhist monk and teacher Thich Nhat Hanh on a talking tour of the United States at the height of the Vietnam War and was impressed how the other managed to respond calmly and peacefully to aggressive verbal attacks from audience members.[11] He wrote a highly regarded biography of Thomas Merton called 'Living with Wisdom'.[12] He later converted to Russian Orthodoxy and is still active in peace issues as the International Secretary of the Orthodox Peace Fellowship. He has published several books on peace and justice issues as well as, more recently, Orthodoxy.

- See http://incommunion.org for further information.

George Fox (1624-1691): Fox was born in Leicestershire, of humble beginnings, during a tumultuous period of English history. Employed as a leather worker, he was intensely disillusioned with the nature of the Christianity he encountered, mainly in the form of the established church. At some stage, he came to an awareness of an 'inner voice' which led him to believe that he, and all individuals, could experience God directly, without anyone, such as a priest, mediating this relationship.[13] He travelled the country, imparting this message and challenging others. His followers became known as 'Friends' and soon became persecuted for their beliefs. Fox earned many enemies through his rejection of oaths, hierarchy, violence and war and spent much time in prison. He and his followers were nick-named Quakers and this name has endured till the present for the Society of Friends. Quakers, with their emphasis on the 'Inner Light', incorporated silence into their collective worship.[14] Fox continued to spread his message throughout England and the Americas, despite ill health, right up until his death. Despite constant persecution and imprisonment, he never wavered from the principle of non-violence.

- See www.quakersintheworld.org for further information.

Pope Francis (1936-): Born in Argentina, Jorge Mario Bergoglio joined the Jesuits and was ordained in 1969. He became Archbishop of Buenos Aires in 1998 and Cardinal in 2001. He became the surprise successor to Pope Benedict the Sixteenth in 2013. He chose the name Francis not after fellow-Jesuit Francis Xavier, but after St. Francis Assisi and this gave a clue to the type of papacy he would instigate. He insists his will be a pastoral papacy rather than a hierarchical and bureaucratic one and he appears keen to get as close as possible to ordinary people as someone in his role can. This approach seems to have endeared him to many, even those without any religious faith. He has a reputation for simplicity and humility and attaches particular importance to gestures, such as washing the feet of prisoners. He instigated a Jubilee Year of Mercy in 2015, when 'Doors of Mercy' were opened in churches around the world to symbolise a more open approach to forgiveness. This does not mean that he is not prepared to confront issues directly and he has made enemies such as some hard-line Catholic traditionalists and governments such as that of Turkey who were outraged by his recognition and highlighting of the Armenian genocide. He also published a papal encyclical on caring for the environment which encourages churches to engage with ecological issues. In 2016, Francis visited Lesbos in Greece, along with Ecumenical Patriarch Bartholomew the First, and returned to the Vatican with a small group of refugees aboard his plane. He tries to maintain good relations with both the Protestant and Orthodox branches of Christianity, as well as with other faiths. Up until now, his papacy seems to be one that tackles social injustice, tries to build bridges with others and promotes peace and environmental awareness.

- See http://m.vaticana.va for further information.

St. Francis of Assisi (1182-1226): Possibly the greatest loved of the Christian saints, Francis had a comfortable start in life as the son of a cloth merchant. After a spiritual crisis, he rejected his military career, which was wrongly interpreted by some as cowardice. While praying at a derelict chapel he heard a voice, which he believed to be that of God, telling him to repair his church. He misinterpreted this as repairing the chapel he was at, but after completing this task saw that it meant to repair the Church in a spiritual sense. He dissociated himself with his wealthy background, dressed in a plain robe, did manual work and aided the poor and sick. This led to notoriety and ridicule, but also to the founding of a dedicated community of followers. In 1210 Pope Innocent the Third gave his approval to the Franciscan order based on poverty and simplicity. He was before his time in championing the welfare of the poor and in advocating respect for all creation. He is famous for his love of animals. He travelled to the Middle East and met with the Sultan of Egypt. Although he tried to convert the Sultan, it was still an early example of peaceful interfaith encounter. For Francis, any encounter of this kind needed to be non-violent as 'he rejected all violence as an offense against the gospel commandment of love and a desecration of God's image in all human beings'.[15] His feast day is the 4th of October and the occasion is sometimes used for the blessing of animals. Francis is also recognised as the patron saint of ecology.

- See www.catholic.org for more information.

Elizabeth Fry (1780-1845): Elizabeth Fry came from a wealthy but not particularly devout Quaker background in Norwich. As she grew older she had a more direct experience of faith and after meeting an American abolitionist decided she wanted to live a life of service to others. However, after marrying Joseph Fry, she ended up bearing eleven children and felt her real vocation was passing her by. She became a visitor to the notorious Newgate prison and was appalled by the conditions she found there. She dedicated the rest of her life to prison reform and sought more humane conditions for those in

England's prisons. Together with other Quaker women, Fry campaigned for a better environment, improved diet and productive activity and managed to achieve many of these things.[16] Perhaps her biggest achievement was to get the public to acknowledge the humanity of those behind bars. Some accused her of prioritising this work at the expense of her family, but her diary entries confirm her concern for her children needs as well as her concern for the welfare of prisoners and that she tried to balance these responsibilities to the best of her ability.[17]

• See www.quakersintheworld.org for further information.

M.K. Gandhi (1869-1948) (Honorary Mention): Gandhi, obviously, was not a Christian but it would have been impossible not to include him due to the influence of Christian ideals on his life and due to the deep impact his example had on Christian pacifists and peacemakers. Martin Luther King [18] stated how much his pacifism was shaped by Gandhi and goes on to claim that 'Gandhi was probably the first person in history to lift the love ethic of Jesus above the mere interaction between individuals to a powerful and effective social force on a large scale'. In 1888, Gandhi went to London to study law and came into contact with many Christian ideas and individuals there. While practising law in South Africa, he experienced first-hand the effects of discriminatory legislation and became politically active for the first time. He returned to India and worked with the Indian National Congress to try to gain independence from British rule. He believed in achieving this through non-violent means only and also endeavoured to use these means to achieve unity between India's diverse cultural and religious groups including 'untouchables', Sikhs, Muslims, Zoroastrians, Christians and Buddhists. Despite this, he could not prevent the country from splitting in a 'Hindu' India and a 'Muslim' Pakistan on being granted independence. Some of the first Christians that Gandhi met in London failed to move him because of their fundamentalist beliefs.[19] Later he came in contact with more open-minded Christians who accepted him for who he was and also awakened in him an interested in comparative religion. William Shirer, who personally knew him, states [20] that Gandhi loved the New Testament and especially the Sermon on the Mount. Gandhi states that he came to believe that his own religion was a religion of service to others and that 'God could be realised only through service'.[21] Gandhi was also deeply influenced by Tolstoy, especially the impassioned pacifism of 'The Kingdom of God is Within You', which he claimed 'overwhelmed' him and 'left an abiding impression.'[22] The career of Gandhi was too long, varied and complex to go into in any great detail here, but the effect that he had on Christian pacifists and peacemakers in subsequent generations cannot be underestimated.

- See www.gandhiheritageportal.org and Gandhi: 2001 for further information.

Khalil Gibran (1883-1931): Gibran was born in Lebanon and emigrated to Boston with his family at the age of twelve. Three of his family died of TB and only his sister Mariana and Khalil survived. His artistic talents were recognised early and by his early twenties he was exhibiting his work. His literary talent emerged a little later. He started by writing for Arabic publications in Boston as he was still not fluent enough to write in English. While studying in Paris he met and sketched Rodin, Yeats and Abdu'l-Baha, son of the founder of the Baha'i faith, who greatly influenced him with his message of unity. He began to publish in English by World War One and published his most famous book 'The Prophet' in 1923. Raised a Maronite Christian, Gibran was never a pacifist but was a peacebuilder in terms of striving towards religious unity. Through his experiences in Lebanon, Paris and the U.S., Gibran was exposed to a vast array of influences. He greatly respected Abdu'l-Baha and his

Baha'i faith which recognises the prophets of all the major religions and promotes a fusing of faiths. Other influences included the Bible, William Blake, Ralph Waldo Emerson and the Romantic Poets along with Hinduism, Buddhism and Sufism.[23] Although a Christian, he was also influenced by Muslim and Arabic culture. He was put off by the machinations of the churches but was attached to the Gospels and greatly admired the person of Jesus and the Sermon on the Mount. Waterfield [24] comments that 'one of his later books, Jesus the Son of Man, picked up the theme that Christ came to help the poor, not found a worldly, wealthy organisation.' Bushrui highlights how through Gibran's universalist approach, he 'endeavours to show how opposites can be reconciled'. Gibran's work produces many elements that are conducive to the promotion of peace including the synthesising of different perspectives and the focus on unity. There is a beauty, exoticism and universalism in his work which inspires harmony. The leading recognised authority on Gibran's work was Suheil Bushrui, a Baha'i, who was Professor and Director of the Khalil Gibran Chair of Values and Peace at Maryland University.

- See http://leb.net/gibran for further information.

Bede Griffiths (1906-1994): Bede Griffiths qualifies as a major Christian peacemaker through becoming almost an embodiment of inter-religious dialogue. Born Alan Richard Griffiths, he claimed he had a mystical experience as a child, the memory and effect of which stayed with him and which he viewed as 'one of the decisive moments of my life'.[25] He was not particularly religious growing up though but became so inclined after graduating from Oxford, through reading Christian spiritual classics and leading a frugal life in a cottage in the Cotswolds. He converted to Roman Catholicism in 1932 and entered the Benedictine Prinknash Abbey soon afterwards.[26] Although his first two decades as a monk were relatively conventional, in the nineteen-fifties Griffiths agreed to go to India to set up a monastery there. He was profoundly moved by the country's spirituality. He realised his calling was to facilitate dialogue between Western and Eastern religion, rather than to teach the Western version of Christianity to Indians. He founded a monastery in Kerala modelled on the traditional Indian ashram and where the barefoot monks wore saffron robes and slept on the floor. Du Boulay [27] states that they 'lived a Cistercian interpretation of the Benedictine Rule, practiced the liturgy of the Syrian Church, and honoured the tradition of the Indian sannyasi'. He studied the Hindu scriptures, meditated and practised yoga. He remained a Christian but tried to re-envisage Christ from an Eastern perspective. He believed in a genuine dialogue between faiths, where Christians and Hindus could meet and engage on an equal footing. He also travelled extensively to try and make Christians more aware of the mystical and contemplative dimension of their faith. He affiliated his ashrams to the Camaldoli order, whose way of life appealed to him.[28] Griffiths is remembered as a renowned teacher of the best of Western spirituality and the best of Eastern spirituality and how these two traditions can be mutually supportive. Although always coming from a Christian perspective, he believed in the equality of the world's religions claiming 'God has graced every tradition with insight into the divine mystery, from the most primitive to the most sophisticated – each has a gift to bring to the world.'[29] In 1968 Griffiths took over the leadership of an ashram in Tamil Nadu, transforming it into a scared space for dialogue and 'the way he bridged Hinduism and Christianity, experiencing all religions as complementary rather than in competition, made Shantivanam a place where people of different religious traditions could meet in an atmosphere of prayer.'[30]

• See www.bedegriffiths.com for further information.

Dag Hammarskjold (1905-1961): Hammarskjold was a Secretary General to the United Nations, who died in a plane crash in Africa while trying to negotiate a solution to violence in the Congo. He had a reputation as a man of principle, but it was only on the discovery of his journals after his death that people became aware of the extent to which his private Christianity motivated him.[31] He provides an ideal example of those many individuals moved by their faith, whatever it may be, both to serve others and to promote the cause of peace.

- See http://www.daghammarsjold.se for further information.

Ammon Hennacy (1893-1970): Hennacy was born in Ohio, USA and in 1917 was sentenced to five years in Atlanta Penitentiary for conscientious objection. During the two years that he served, he underwent a religious conversion and came to a realisation of the radical message of Jesus and that what mattered was the 'one-man revolution' that can take place in each individual's heart. Hennacy described himself as a Christian anarchist, becoming vegetarian, living a simple life and refusing to pay taxes which could be used to fund war. He worked on the land, earning below the taxable minimum to achieve this. He joined the New York Catholic Worker community in 1952, encouraging it to become more engaged with peace work and he took a strong anti-nuclear stance. He converted to Catholicism but later disengaged with the church because it didn't adopt a strong enough anti-war stance, though he continued to identify as Christian. He opened a house of hospitality in Salt Lake City called Joe Hill House and fasted every year to express regret at the dropping of the nuclear bombs in 1945. He died while undertaking such a protest in 1970. Ellsberg [32] quotes him as saying: 'Love without courage and wisdom is sentimentality, as with the ordinary church member. Courage without love and wisdom is foolhardiness, as with the ordinary soldier. Wisdom without love and courage is cowardice, as with the ordinary intellectual. The one who has love, courage and wisdom is one in a million, who moves the world, as with Jesus, Buddha and Gandhi'.

- See www.catholicworker.org for further information.

Henry Hodgkin (1877-1933): Henry Hodgkin was a doctor, Quaker and pacifist from Co. Durham. He studied at Cambridge and completed his medical training at St. Thomas' Hospital in London before becoming a missionary in China. After returning to England in 1910, Hodgkin became more active in promoting peace and attended a conference of Christian pacifists in southern Germany in 1914. War broke out while this conference was being held and Hodgkin vowed with a German Lutheran pastor he met that they would always be 'one in Christ'. As a Quaker, this implied that he needed to refrain from participating in the war but was also duty-bound to come up with ways of actively promoting peace. He convened a meeting of pacifists in Cambridge the same year and the Fellowship of Reconciliation was born, a pacifist organisation active and influential to this day. Hodgkin rightly became its first president. In 1929 he helped to found the Quaker Pendle Hill Centre near Philadelphia, where he remained till 1932. Hodgkin died the following year.

- See www.for.org.uk for further information.

Trevor Huddleston (1913-1998): After studying at Oxford and Wells Theological College, Huddleston joined the Anglican Community of the Resurrection and was posted to Johannesburg, South Africa, where he gained a reputation both as a highly respected priest and campaigner against racial discrimination and the Apartheid system. He worked tirelessly to improve the lot of black children in educational and social terms and was a formative influence on Desmond Tutu. He received the Indira Gandhi Award for Peace, Disarmament and Development and after his death Huddleston

Centres for disabled youths were established in Hackney, East London and Sophiatown, Johannesburg.

- See www.trevorhuddleston.org for further information.

Catherine de Hueck Doherty: Catherine de Hueck Doherty was born in Russia but raised a Catholic. She served as a nurse during the First World War, while her Baron husband fought at the front. After the 1917 Revolution, they escaped to Canada. Catherine travelled on to New York, where she strangely secured a job lecturing about her personal experiences. Her marriage broke down, but she was now quite well off in her own right. She was troubled by this material comfort and made a choice to reject her wealth and move to a poor area of Toronto. She set up Friendship House there, with the support of the local archbishop, to provide help to the homeless and those in need. Later, she set up a Friendship House in New York, where she also sought to break down barriers between blacks and whites. She received support from Dorothy Day in her endeavours and was also a formative influence on a young Thomas Merton. She believed that if Gospel values were properly implemented, Communism would lose all its appeal and influence. She later married Eddie Doherty, a journalist, and resigned her role at Friendship House. They established a new community, called Madonna House, in rural Ontario, where she tried to live a life of prayer coupled with a commitment to promoting justice.[33]

- See www.madonnahouse.org for further information.

Franz Jagerstatter (1907-1943): Jagerstatter was an ordinary family man who lived in Austria during the Nazi occupation and who was conscripted in 1943. As a conscientious objector, he refused to serve, was arrested and subsequently beheaded as 'an enemy of state'.[34] Although many, including his parish priest and family, had tried to dissuade him from this course of action, Jagerstatter, who was both committed to his Catholicism and a man of high principle, concluded that he had no alternative. Prior to his execution, he was given several opportunities to recant, but he stuck to what he believed was the right thing to do. Unfortunately, he did not receive the support he deserved from the Austrian church and then as now individuals have sometimes proved more principled than the institutions they belong to.

• See Ellsberg: 2000 for further information.

Bruce Kent (1929 -): Bruce Kent became involved in peace issues, after being ordained a Roman Catholic priest in the late 1950's, when he was asked to become chaplain to the British Section of Pax Christi. [35] He served as both General Secretary and Chair of the Campaign for Nuclear Disarmament (CND) throughout the 1980's. His involvement with CND took a great personal toll as he was vilified as a communist sympathiser and his relationship with the Catholic hierarchy became increasingly strained. He has also served as Chair of War on Want and President of the International Peace Bureau. He emphasises co-operation between religions as a central requirement for a peaceful society.[36] He left the priesthood in order to stand in the 1987 General Election when he failed to become an MP and he later married. He has continued to be actively involved in peace issues well into his eighties and still gives talks and has letters published in the media.

• See http://bruce-kent.com for more details.

Cardinal Stephen Kim Sou-hwan (1922-2009): Having previously been Archbishop of Seoul, at 46 years old Kim became the youngest person to have been elevated to the College of Cardinals in 1969. During the 1970's and 1980's the Catholic church played a central role in the Korean movement for democracy and Kim Sou-Han was prominent in this process. On one occasion, he refused to hand over to the military authorities, pro-democracy protesters who were sheltering in his Cathedral. At the time government critics were being kidnapped and tortured. He was criticised by some in the Church as being overly politicised but those who knew him say that he was motivated solely by his faith to show concern for the human rights of others.[37]

- See McKitterick: The Independent: 21/09/2009 (www.independent.co.uk) for further details.

Martin Luther King, Jr. (1929-1968): Martin Luther King is an undisputed heavyweight in terms of Christian peacemaking and non-violence. He was born and raised in the Southern U.S. state of Georgia. On completion of his school education, he left the South for a number of years to study and completed a Degree in Sociology, a B. Div. degree and a Doctorate in Theology. During this time, he scrutinised the ideas of such diverse thinkers as Marx, Aristotle, Betham, Mill, Locke, Raschenbusch and Niebuhr and engaged with modern methods of biblical criticism. He flirted with Agnosticism and Liberal Christianity but identified flaws in both. Two of the people who influenced him most were Thoreau, especially his 'On Civil Disobedience', and Gandhi and eventually he developed his own individual perspective on things.

On completion of his studies, he had a number of job offers but eventually opted for a pastoral role with a Baptist church in Montgomery, Alabama. This choice sealed his fate, as due to his character and integrity, he was unable to decline playing a leading role in the political events that unfolded there. Segregation between whites and blacks was still in force in Alabama and this was challenged in 1955 when Rosa Parks, a black woman, got arrested after sitting on a 'whites only' seat at the front of a bus and refusing to move. In reaction to her arrest, a boycott of buses by blacks was led by King, culminating in the overturning of segregation on Montgomery buses by the supreme court. Throughout this trying and frightening time, when blacks were frequently harassed, threatened and arrested, King pleaded with his followers to refrain from violence and to respond only with love. He attributed his approach to putting Christian principles into action through Gandhian non-violence. His previous intellectual endeavours had culminated in a simple, practical and effective approach. He went on to lead subsequent protests in the South and helped organise the March on Washington in 1963 where he gave his famous 'I have a dream' speech. He advocated against segregated housing in Chicago and also opposed American involvement in the war in Vietnam.

With some of the people in this section, I was unsure whether or not to include them, as it was sometimes difficult to gauge the extent to which their Christianity guided their actions. I did not face this dilemma with King, whose own words leave us in no doubt about where his motivation stemmed from. Towards the end of his career, a more radical King had emerged 'who criticised the war in Vietnam and who voiced doubts over the ability of capitalism to deliver social and economic justice'.[38] In contrasting Christianity with Marxism around this time King stated 'The great tragedy is that Christianity failed to see that it had the revolutionary edge. You don't have to go to Karl Marx to learn how to be a revolutionary. I didn't get my inspiration from Marx; I got it from a man named Jesus, a Galilean saint who said he was anointed to heal the broken-hearted. He was anointed to deal with the problems of the poor. And that is where we get our inspiration'.[39] And, of course, through all of this, King did not waver at any time from non-violence.

He was assassinated in Memphis on April 4th, 1968. The day before, he had delivered a speech which had proven to be eerily prophetic. Part of it is quoted below:

'Well, I don't know what will happen now. We've got some difficult days ahead. But it doesn't matter with me now. Because I have been to the mountaintop. And I don't mind. Like anybody, I would like to live a long life. Longevity has its place. But I am not concerned about that now. I just want to do God's will. And he has allowed me to go up the mountain. And I have looked over. And I have seen the promised land. I may not get there with you. But I want you to know tonight that we, as a people, will get to the promised land. So, I am happy tonight. I am not worried about anything. I'm not fearing any man. Mine eyes have seen the coming of the Lord'.

The words of this quote are inspirational, but to hear the recording of King speaking them is an intensely moving experience and in itself is a fitting tribute to his and his community's achievement. King was awarded the Nobel Peace Prize in 1964, the Congressional Gold Medal after his death and Martin Luther King Day became a Federal National Holiday in 1986.

- See http://thekingcenter.org for further information.

Hans Kung (1928 -): Swiss-born Kung, a theologian, participated at the Second Vatican Council in an advisory capacity. He had his licence to teach Roman Catholic theology at Tubingen University revoked in 1971 after denying the doctrine of papal infallibility. He was subsequently kept on at Tubingen as Professor of Ecumenical Theology and gained a reputation as an authority on world religions.[40] In 1993, Kung initiated his Global Ethic project and the 'Towards a Global Ethic' document was signed at the World

46

Parliament of Religions by eminent spiritual leaders such as the Dalai Lama. The Declaration tried to steer a middle course between being too political or too religious and endeavoured to encourage the major world religions to emphasise core shared values such as forgiveness, non-violence and equality [42] He has received numerous awards including the Karl Barth Prize, the Interfaith Gold Medallion from the International Council of Christianity and Judaism, the German Order of Merit, the Niwano Peace Prize and the Otto Hahn Peace Medal for his contribution to global ethics and the promotion of dialogue between religions.

- See Kung: 2002 for further information.

Mairead Maguire (nee Corrigan) (1944-): Maguire helped found the Women for Peace movement in Northern Ireland, which later became known as the Community of Peace People, as a non-violent response to the ongoing conflict there. She won the Nobel Peace Prize in 1976, along with Betty Williams, for these efforts. She is a firm believer in tackling the causes of violence through education. From the nineteen-eighties onwards she became more involved in a wider range of issues including the fate of political prisoners worldwide, opposing war and nuclear weapons and has been especially vocal on the Israeli-Palestinian conflict. She is very supportive of nuclear whistle-blower Mordechai Vananu and critical of the treatment he has received from the Israeli authorities. She has made herself unpopular in the US through her opposition to military action in Afghanistan and Iraq and through her criticism of President Obama, a fellow Nobel Laureate, for his failure to reduce US military aggression and his avoidance of the Dalai Lama. She is an admirer of Gandhi's philosophy of non-violence and also believes in interfaith dialogue as a means of overcoming division. However, despite denials of ill intent, many of her statements about Israel have been perceived as distasteful, if not potentially harmful.

- See www.nobelprize.org for further information.

Peter Maurin (1877-1949): Maurin, a co-founder of the Catholic Worker Movement with Dorothy Day, was born in France but eventually settled in New York. In his forties, Maurin gained a new-found interest in his Catholic faith, inspired by the example of St. Francis of Assisi. He began to only charge what students could afford for the French lessons he gave them. He got to know Dorothy Day and encouraged her to start a newspaper to promote Catholic thought, which was named the Catholic Worker. Together they founded 'houses of hospitality' for the urban poor and communal farms in rural areas. Maurin toured widely, giving talks to promote the ideas of the movement, before dying in 1949. He believed that society's problems lay in the fact that 'sociology, economics and politics had all been separated from the Gospels' and they need to be reintegrated in order to heal the divisions in community.[43] Dorothy Day claims that she would never have been able to start the Catholic Worker had it not been for Maurin's help and encouragement.

- See www.catholicworker.org for further information.

Thomas Merton (1915-1968): Before entering the Trappist order, Thomas Merton led a very varied and, at times, unsettled life. His father was a painter from New Zealand and his mother a Quaker. His early life was nomadic and he went to school in England and France before studying at Columbia University.[44] He lost both parents before reaching adulthood. He was not religious growing up but visits to churches in Rome made an impression on him. He developed a reputation as a womanizer in in Cambridge and is thought to have fathered an illegitimate child there. He became a Catholic in 1938 while studying at Columbia University. He tried to join the Franciscan order but was rejected by them as unsuitable.

While trying to discern what to do next he got a job lecturing and also volunteered at Friendship House in Harlem which opened his eyes to the true extent of poverty in the area. In 1941, he entered the Trappist Abbey of Gethsemani in Kentucky. He was a prolific writer and in 1948 published 'The Seven Story Mountain' which became a bestseller and gained him a reputation as a spiritual writer. He wrote on a wide variety of topics which included mystical theology, spirituality, different religions especially Buddhism, peace and social justice issues as well as being a poet and prolific journal writer. He always found it difficult to fit into monastic life and longed for more solitude. Eventually, he was allowed to move into a hermitage on the Abbey's grounds. In 1968 he was allowed to undertake a tour of Asia, which was a dream come true for him. He met the Dalai Lama in India and the Dalai Lama himself still expresses the importance of this meeting for him. Unfortunately, Merton died after being electrocuted by an electric fan during this trip. Although, many remembered Merton for his first book, 'The Seven Storey Mountain', 'later in life Merton became increasingly interested in in Eastern thought, developing great respect for Zen Buddhism and Taoist philosophy'.[45] He remained deeply committed to his Christian faith but was a great advocate of interfaith understanding. Merton was also involved in many peace and justice issues and was committed to non-violence and critical of those who took an extreme or aggressive approach. He believed that genuine Christianity required a renunciation of violence.[46] Because he was physically prevented from active participation in non-violent actions, his relationship with the peace movement was mainly dependant on correspondence with those involved and through publication about peace issues.

- See http://merton.org for further information.

Henry Nouwen (1932 -1996): Henry Nouwen was a Dutch-born priest who carved out a very unconventional career through following his intuition even when this meant being completely truthful and acknowledging his own vulnerability. As a result, he became a greatly admired and loved spiritual writer. After ordination Nouwen moved to the U.S. where he was a successful lecturer in Notre Dame and Yale. He gained a popular following through writing such books as 'Wounded Healer', but he still felt out-of-place in the world. In 1974 he spent some time in a Trappist monastery to further explore his spiritual side and then, a number of years later, lived among the poor of Bolivia and Peru. He realised that he was not suited to this particular life and returned to North America to lecture at Harvard Divinity School. Despite his outward success at this, he was still trying to discern his true vocation and eventually found it living in a L'Arche community for people with learning disabilities. He appeared to be much happier doing this, but also continued to write prolifically and his books have remained popular ever since.[47] Despite being renowned for being a writer of popular spirituality, Nouwen also maintained an underlying commitment to peace and justice. John Dear highlights this in an article in the National Catholic Reporter.[48] Dear quotes Nouwen as saying that 'for Jesus, there are no countries to be conquered, no ideologies to be imposed, no people to be dominated', and that 'there are only children, women and men to be loved'. This gentle brand of non-violence did not stop him from engagement with peace work. Dear describes how Nouven used to write to him when he, Dear, was serving an eight-month sentence for non-violent action at an air force base. He reminds us that Nouwen marched with Martin Luther King, addressed anti-war rallies, hosted Masses for anti-nuclear protesters, opposed U.S. interference in South and Central America, visited the Berrigan brothers in jail and protested against the first Gulf War. He believed that Jesus was unconditionally committed to peacemaking and that no Christian can be excused from being supportive of this. He also advocated rooting this process in contemplative prayer. Dear concludes that Nouwen's perspective demands that 'work for disarmament and justice' is 'integral to the life of every authentic Christian'.

- See http://henrinouwen.org for more details.

Paul Oestreicher (1931-): Oestreicher was born in Germany but grew up in New Zealand as his family had to flee Nazi persecution due to his father's Jewish ancestry. He studied in Germany after the war and worked as a pastor at a German church for a while in the 1950's. He was ordained in the Church of England in 1960. He worked in a number of London churches, for the BBC's religious department and for the British Council of Churches. While director of Amnesty UK he campaigned for political prisoners in Eastern Europe. He also maintained a strong connection with Germany and supported its reunification. In the 1980's he joined the Quakers as well as working as Director for Coventry Cathedral's Reconciliation Centre. After retirement, he continued to write journalistic pieces on peace and social justice issues.

- See The Friend: 17/02/2006 for further information.

William Penn (1644-1718): William Penn was an English Quaker who was the founder of the colony of Pennsylvania. He managed to achieve this after King Charles the Second gave his father a huge tract of land to satisfy an outstanding debt. On his arrival there in 1682, the existing settlers pledged their allegiance to Penn who set up a general assembly to govern and founded the capital, Philadelphia. Penn advocated for the separate English colonies there to unite and Pennsylvania's system of government was an inspiration for the American Constitution. Penn became a Quaker in his early twenties against his families wishes. He became close to George Fox and travelled with him in England and Europe and at the same time contributing to adding structure to the Quaker faith. He was imprisoned many times and wrote texts which were critical of the religious and political establishment. When he founded his colony, he hoped it could provide not just a refuge for persecuted Quakers but also become a haven of tolerance, democracy and religious freedom. Among the persecuted minorities attracted to Pennsylvania were Catholics, Jews, Huguenots, Mennonites and Amish from different areas of Europe. He set up trial by jury and tried to make the prison system humane. Penn returned to England in 1684 and only came back to Pennsylvania at the end of the century. He found the colony to be thriving with a growing and well-educated population. Unfortunately, many Quakers, including Penn, still owned slaves, but attitudes towards that practice were changing gradually. He returned once more to England where he was plagued by debts. He tried without success to sell off his colony and died penniless in 1718.

- See www.penntreatymuseum.org for further information.

Sr. Helen Prejean (1939-): Helen Prejean became a nun in 1957 and has been engaged in education most of her working life. Her life took an unusual turn when she started to correspond with a convicted murderer on 'Death Row'. After visiting him, she agreed to become his spiritual advisor and witnessed his last months at close hand right up to his execution. This experience deeply affected her and she committed herself to campaigning for the abolition of the death penalty, as well as ministering to others on 'Death Row'. To counterbalance this, she also advocated for proper support for the victims of violent crime. A book and a film starring Susan Sarandon, entitled 'Dead Man Walking', recounts the experiences of Prejean's 'Death Row' ministry. Prejean received many honorary degrees and awards for her work including the Pax Christi USA Pope Paul IV Teacher of Peace Award and the Pacem in Terris Award.

- See www.sisterhelen.org for further information.

Pandita Ramabai (1858-1922): Pandita Ramabai was raised a Hindu and given a very comprehensive education for a Indian female of the time. After the death of her family in a famine, the young Ramabai travelled across India and greatly impressed people with her knowledge. After becoming more aware of child marriage and the conditions of widows, she campaigned vigorously against them as well as setting up educational centres for widows and orphans. She came into contact with Christian missionaries and eventually became a Christian herself, believing that service to the poor was a religious duty. She came under criticism from Indians for a perceived rejection of her culture and from Christians for not been doctrinally orthodox enough.[49] She worked tirelessly both to bridge these two faiths and to advocate justice for women, children and the poor.

- See Ellsberg: 2000 for further information.

Donald Reeves (1935-): Donald Reeves is an Anglican clergyman who is perceived as something of a rebel by his contemporaries and was labelled a 'very dangerous man' by Margaret Thatcher. After finishing at Cambridge University, he worked for a time in Beirut before training as a priest. He was influenced by liberal churchmen such as Bishop John Robinson and was attracted to urban ministry, working in London's East End before transferring to St. James Church, Piccadilly in central London. He was credited with the greatly increased renown and popularity of this church through implementing a policy of trying to make everyone as welcome as possible there. He transformed it into a forum for political debate and engagement, with left-wingers such as Tony Benn and right-wingers like Michael Heseltine speaking there. Disturbed by the ethnic violence in Bosnia and the wider Balkan area, Reeves founded an organisation called Soul of Europe to try to bring the diverse factions together. He titled his autobiography 'Memoirs of a Very Dangerous Man'.[50] Reeves states: 'You don't make peace through talking to your friends; you have to make peace with your enemies.'

- See http://verydangerousman.wordpress.com for further information.

Oscar Romero (1917-1980): Oscar Romero was elected Archbishop of San Salvador in 1977 and started out in this role as a very conservative and uncritical pastor. El Salvador was in a state of chaos and violence during this period and Romero appears to have undergone a deep transformation as the result of the murder of another priest who was a friend and also through becoming more attuned to the many injustices around him.[51] He began to use his weekly sermons to speak out against poverty, torture and assassination, courageously denouncing these outrages and making many enemies in this dangerous and deeply divided society. He wrote to Jimmy Carter of the U.S., asking the government there to stop sending arms to the El Salvadoran regime. The next day, 24th March, 1980, he was gunned down at the alter while saying mass and died very shortly afterwards. He provides a good example of a Christian who didn't deliberately seek out a role in peacebuilding, but was diverted into it through circumstances and through facing up to his conscience. He was beatified by Pope Francis on 23rd May, 2015. He is also respected beyond the frontiers of Roman Catholicism; US. President, Barack Obama, visited his tomb in 2011 and he is depicted in relief at the front of the Anglican Westminster Abbey in London.

- See www.romerotrust.org.uk for further information.

Michel Sabbah (1933 -): Michel Sabbah served as Latin Patriarch of Jerusalem between 1987 and 2008. He was the first Palestinian to hold this role in recent times. The Latin Patriarch is the head of the Roman Catholics (who are mainly Palestinian Arabs) in Israel and the Palestinian Territories. Prior to becoming Patriarch, Sabbah worked as a parish priest, studied in Lebanon and the Sorbonne, taught in Djibouti and served as President of the University of Bethlehem. In the role of Latin Patriarch, he was an outspoken advocate for Palestinian rights and a critic of the security wall and the Israeli occupation of the West Bank and Gaza. He was also President of Pax Christi International during much of this time.

- See Hilliard and Bailey: 1999 for further information.

Albert Schweitzer (1875-1965): Albert Schweitzer was one of the great polymaths of the twentieth century, excelling in philosophy, theology and music before, at the age of thirty, embarking on a medical degree to allow him to do missionary work in Africa. Although a Lutheran curate, he held some very unorthodox theological views regarding the person of Jesus which he expounded in The Mystery of the Kingdom of God. This put him at odds with the church authorities, but did not stop him proceeding with his medical work in Africa, which he continued until his death at the age of ninety. He tried to live a life based on the principles of loving God, loving your neighbour and showing reverence for all live. He was awarded the Nobel peace prize in 1952 and used the occasion to promote peace and to oppose nuclear weapons.[52]

- See www.schweitzer.org for further information.

Dick Sheppard (1880-1937): Dick Sheppard was an Anglican priest and a pacifist. After ordination, he went to work with the poor in the East End of London but had a breakdown due to his heavy workload. He served as chaplain to a military hospital in France during the First World War but again suffered from burnout and was sent home. He

55

then became the resident priest for the high-profile St. Martins-in-the-Fields, Trafalgar Square but resigned for health reasons in 1926. He was appointed as Dean of Canterbury in 1929 where he was popular but had to resign again in 1931 for health reasons. Always committed to his pacifist principles, he established the Peace Pledge Union in 1936 to encourage individuals to dedicate themselves to the cause of peace. He died in 1937 and was buried at Canterbury Cathedral. He wrote extensively, often on the subject of peace and his publications include 'We Say No: The Plain Man's Guide to Pacifism' (1935) and 'Let Us Honour Peace' (1937).

- See www.ppu.org.uk for further information.

Menno Simons (1496-1561): Simons, who had previously been a Catholic priest, was a prominent Anabaptist leader in the Low Countries at a time when the group was split between those individuals who rejected violence and those who did not. His brother was killed while taking part in the takeover of a monastery by a group of violent Anabaptists. Menno then had a spiritual crisis before being instrumental in uniting many of the diverse Anabaptist groups through the acceptance of pacifist principles.[53] The emerging Mennonites, as they were called, embraced not just pacifism but also a life governed by simplicity and a certain amount of detachment from the world.

- See http://www.mennosimons.net for further information.

St. Maria Skobtsova of Paris (1891-1945): Originally named Elizaverta (Liza) Pilenko, she grew up in pre-revolutionary Russia in a devout Orthodox family. As a teenager, she developed an atheistic perspective after the death of her father. As a young adult with a strong sense of justice, she gravitated towards left-wing and radical causes and lived a Bohemian lifestyle in St. Petersburg. Her first marriage failed, but not before she gave birth to a daughter. As well as being politically involved, she wrote poetry and studied theology, which led her back to the Orthodoxy of her youth. After the revolution, she fled Russia with her second husband Daniel Sokbtsova, finally arriving in Paris in 1923. As her second marriage faltered, she became more involved with her faith and the Russian Christian Student Movement. In 1932 she became an Orthodox nun, known after as Mother Maria. Maria opened a house of hospitality in Paris for the poor and dispossessed. Due to its popularity, she soon required and opened a larger property staffed by dedicated volunteers. She opened a sanatorium for Russian exiles suffering from TB. Along with some other Christians, she helped found Orthodox Action which provided a wider range of social services to the Russian émigré community. She voluntarily stayed on in Paris after the Nazi invasion, as she was not prepared to abandon those whom she helped. Many, including Russians, perceived as enemies by the Germans, were arrested and Mother Maria set out to provide aid to them. When thousands of Jews were rounded up and held in a sports stadium, Mother Maria went there to bring food and comfort, as well as managing to rescue several children. She gave refuge to many more in her house of hospitality. Eventually, she too was arrested and spent the last two years of her life in Ravensbruck concentration camp. On the 30th of March, 1945, Mother Maria died in the gas chambers and was finally recognised as a saint by the Orthodox Church in 2004. She represents an example of an individual who rises to the challenges faced by them in the most noble of ways, always responding in a way that promotes peace and justice.

- See www.incommunion.org for further information.

Lord Donald Soper (1903-1998): Lord Soper was a Methodist minister, as well as being a prominent socialist and pacifist. He was educated at Cambridge and the London School of Economics. From early in his career until a very ripe old age, he preached outdoors at strategic spots in London such as Tower Hill and Speakers Corner in Hyde Park. He became especially renowned for this activity and photographs of him in full flow were easily recognisable. He was comfortable in this role, as well as being entertaining, and he earned the nickname 'Lord Soapbox'. He was based in London for the duration of his career and his socialist principles underlined his ministry and made him critical of some in power such as Margaret Thatcher whose policies he vehemently opposed. He joined Dick Sheppard's Peace Pledge Union in 1937, remained a pacifist during World War Two and campaigned against nuclear weapons in its aftermath. He also served for a number of years as president of the English branch of the Fellowship of Reconciliation. Peel [54] states that Soper's pacifism brought about a 'subtle shift in the Church's attitude towards war and nuclear weapons'.

- See www.ppu.org for further information.

Mother Teresa of Calcutta (1910-1997): Mother Teresa was an Albanian, born in Skopje which is now in Macedonia. Although, she joined the Loreto Sisters and was teaching in India, she experienced a call to do something more unique. She obtained permission to leave her convent to work among the poor in Calcutta and by 1950 had gained so much support from others that she was granted permission by the Vatican to set up her own order, which became known as the Missionaries of Charity. By the end of the century, it had approximately 4,000 members working with people who were disabled, elderly, destitute, orphaned, living with AIDS, addicted to alcohol, terminally ill, refugees, etc. Through the efforts of documentary makers, such as Malcolm Muggeridge, she became well known in the West, attracting both praise and criticism. Muggeridge [55] described how she appeared to be able to transcend cultural, social and religious divisions and states his surprise at seeing her inspire a woman from a high caste to attend to the poverty-stricken. She rebuffed the criticisms, saying that the sole focus of her vocation was to care for others, rather than trying to change social structures. She received the Nobel Prize in 1979, for her efforts to 'overcome poverty and distress in the world, which also constitute a threat to peace' and was canonised as a saint of the Roman Catholic Church in 2016.

• See Ellsberg: 2000 and Muggeridge: 1996 for further information.

Leo Tolstoy (1828-1910): Tolstoy came from a wealthy family, became disillusioned with his Orthodox faith in his teens, served as an officer in the Crimean War, travelled and led a hedonistic lifestyle before settling on his family estate and earning a successful living as a writer. He started practicing his Orthodox faith again, tried to lead a simple life in solidarity with the peasants and wrote on more serious matters. He gradually came to believe that the original message of the Gospels, and in particular the Sermon on the Mount, had become diluted through ritual, dogma and subservience to the state.[56] This was and is particularly evident in the Russian Orthodox Church, which appears to be prone to phyletism or religious nationalism, which was condemned as a form of heresy and racism at the Pan-Orthodox Synod in Constantinople in 1872. Tolstoy was excommunicated in 1901, after having accused the Russian Church of having ethically lost its way. He outlined his views on Christian non-violence in 'The Kingdom of God is Within You' (1894), a book which is said to have greatly influenced Gandhi. In it Tolstoy outlines his view, very simply and forcefully, that the way of violence cannot be in any way compatible with the Christian message, especially that of the Sermon on the Mount. In this book, he put forward his views uncompromisingly – it was both hard-hitting and inspiring. Tolstoy also tried to live out his beliefs and was convinced of the value of a simple life. He showed interest in the cause of Indian independence and expounded his views on this matter in a 'Letter to a Hindoo' (1908), leading to Gandhi corresponding with him. Gandhi named his South African ashram Tolstoy Farm. Tolstoy also corresponded with English and American Quakers and showed interest in their beliefs. He showed interest in and concern for the Doukhobors, a Christian group persecuted for their pacifism and conscientious objection leading to their migration from Russia and Georgia to the relative tolerance of Canada.

- See Bartlett: 2010 for further information.

Desmond Tutu (1931 -): Archbishop Desmond Tutu of Cape Town in South Africa has been a tireless campaigner for peace, racial equality and human rights for decades. In his early life, he met and was deeply influenced by Trevor Huddleston. After being ordained in South Africa, he then studied at theology at Kings College, London before returning to his native land and being appointed Archbishop of Cape Town and Anglican Primate of South Africa in the 1980's. He became an outspoken critic of the Apartheid regime and its inherent racism but always rejected the path of violence. Although a knowledgeable theologian, he was also a pastor skilled in relating to individuals from all social and ethnic backgrounds. While advocating sanctions, he was adamant that white South Africans were as human as anyone else and should not be demonised and he was appreciative of those within the white community who opposed Apartheid, often at personal cost to themselves.[57] He was awarded the Nobel Peace Prize in 1986. He has received countless other accolades including the Albert Schweitzer Prize for Humanitarianism, the Pacem in Terris Award and the Gandhi Peace Prize. After the demise of Apartheid, Tutu headed the Truth and Reconciliation Commission which was intended to heal the fractures in South African society through a process of restorative justice. The Commission looked at human rights abuses on all sides and had the power to grant amnesties for crimes which were politically motivated. Though not without problems, it is thought to have facilitated a relatively smooth transition to a more balanced civil society. Despite Tutu's huge popularity worldwide, he always viewed himself as a churchman rather than a professional politician. His theology is liberal and he is also an outspoken advocate of gay rights and the need to tackle AIDS. People appear to warm to his personality and he is easily recognised by his infectious laugh and sense of joy.

- See www.tutu.org for further information.

Evelyn Underhill (1875-1941): Underhill was an Anglican pacifist and writer who wrote widely on the subject of Christian spirituality. She displayed mystical leanings from a young age and developed a lifelong interest in spirituality which was not shared by her barrister husband. However, after graduating from Kings College, London, she managed to carve out a career for herself writing, lecturing and giving retreats. She wrote both novels and non-fiction dealing with mystical themes. At the end of the nineteen-thirties she joined the Anglican Pacifist Fellowship and wrote a number of anti-war tracts for them. As a pacifist, she was deeply affected by the devastation of World War Two and died in 1942.

- See www.evelynunderhill.org for further information.

Mordechai Vananu (1954 -): Vananu is an Moroccan Israeli who converted from Judaism to Christianity. While working as a nuclear technician, he revealed secret information regarding Israel's nuclear programme to the British press in 1986, stating his opposition to these weapons. He was kidnapped by Israeli secret services in Italy, and after a covert trial, spent 18 years in prison including many in solitary confinement. He has had many restrictions placed on his freedom since his release from prison in 2004, including restrictions on speaking to foreigners. Since his release from prison, he has lived in St. Georges Cathedral in Jerusalem. Attempts to apply for asylum in other countries have not been successful and restrictions continue to be applied. Vananu continues to be defiant and has been at the receiving end of ongoing harassment, arrests and short imprisonments. Even though he was refused asylum in Norway, he has received much support from that country including getting an honorary doctorate from Tromso University and receiving the Peace Prize of the Norwegian People. He has been nominated several times for the Nobel Peace Prize. Vananu continues to be a controversial figure.

- See www.vananu.com for further information.

Jean Vanier (1928-): Jean Vanier is an ex-naval officer known for his founding of L'Arche communities for people with learning disabilities. These communities are based on equality between the people who have the disabilities and the volunteers or assistants who live in the communities with them. There are now communities in several dozen countries worldwide. He has worked ceaselessly to break down the barriers that exist between those with disability and those without disability. Butler [58] points out that although Vanier comes from a Catholic background and the communities were set up with a Christian ethos, the faiths of non-Christians are respected and facilitated in different parts of the world, especially those where Christianity is not a majority, and she describes how the prayer room in the Calcutta community is decorated with the symbols of many faiths. Vanier [59] advises us that it is up to every one of us to promote peace and this task should not be left solely to governments. Vanier has won several awards including the French Legion of Honour, the

Order of Canada, the Pacem in Terris Peace and Freedom Award and the Templeton Prize.

- See Vanier: 2003 for further information.

Terry Waite (1939-): Terry Waite started his career in the Church Army, an Anglican organisation that provides social services. Later he was involved in church training programmes before spending time working for the Anglican Church in Uganda, Rome and Asia. In 1980, he became an assistant to Robert Runcie, Archbishop of Canterbury, travelling with him all over the world. He successfully negotiated the release of a number of Middle East hostages before been taken hostage himself in Lebanon in 1987. He was only released in 1991. After his release, he committed himself to lecturing, writing and promoting social justice issues. He published a number of books including 'Taken on Trust' which dealt with his experience as a hostage and the lighter 'Travels with a Primate' about his time as Robert Runcie's assistant. He is involved in a number of charitable organisations including Hostage UK and Emmaus UK. He joined the Quakers in 2008. He holds honorary degrees from a number of British universities.

- See Waite: 2016 for further information.

Betty Williams (1943-): Williams was awarded the Nobel Peace Prize in 1976 along with Mairead Maguire (nee Corrigan) for their co-founding of the Peace People movement in Northern Ireland to challenge the paramilitary violence there and the effect it had on the civilian population. She was drawn into this arena after witnessing three children killed by a paramilitary making his escape in a speeding car. She started a petition for peace and along with Maguire instigated peace marches which drew up to 30,000 protesters despite opposition from and disruption from the IRA. Their aim was to build a just and peaceful society for themselves and their children. She won several other awards for this work, including the People's Peace Prize of Norway. Williams has stayed active in many organisations and lectures widely on peace and interfaith understanding. She has always appeared to have a special concern for the effect of conflict on children and also lectures on children's rights issues.

- See www.nobelprize.org for further information.

Rowan Williams (1950-): Williams, former Archbishop of Canterbury, is an intellectual heavyweight whose exact views are sometimes difficult to pinpoint due to the elaborate way in which he expresses himself. However, he appears to be able to discern and empathize with different sides of an argument and to favour dialogue and the peaceful reconciliation of opposing parties. He has consistently spoken out against war and injustice and is supportive of strong ecumenical and interfaith relations. Originally from Wales, he gained a strong academic background in Oxford and Cambridge. He has good knowledge of several languages, both ancient and modern, and has published books of poetry as well as his academic works of theology. He was appointed Archbishop of Canterbury in 2002 after a decade as Bishop of Monmouth in Wales. This was an intensely challenging role for him as the Anglican Communion was deeply divided over the issues of women's ordination and gay clergy. To compound this problem, the division appeared to correspond to a divide between a liberal but prosperous North and a traditional but poor South with bishops from the developing world accusing the Europeans and North Americans of trying to foist their decadent values on them. Williams tried, without success, to reconcile these elements at the 2010 Lambeth Conference and ended up attracting criticism from all sides. He attempted this through introducing an 'Anglican Covenant' designed to hold the diffuse elements of the Communion together but not many wholly bought into this idea.

Williams has always shown interest in peace and justice issues and was arrested at a CND protest in 1985. He witnessed the 2001 attacks in New York as he was just a short distance away from the Twin Towers at the time, and he recorded this event in a book of poetry entitled Writing in the Dust. He firmly opposed U.S. and British military action in the Middle East and wrote to Tony Blair outlining his concerns. Williams has a broad theological perspective which has led to a deep ecumenical engagement. He is a great admirer of the Eastern Orthodox tradition and focused on the work of Russian theologian Vladimir Lossky for his Ph.D. He is a patron of the Fellowship of Saint Alban and Saint Sergius which fosters links between Anglican and Orthodox churches. He encouraged dialogue with the Muslim community after the events of 9/11, as well as promoting understanding of other faiths. Although always a peacemaker, he is not quite a pacifist and Shortt [60] points out that Williams showed in his writing that he 'rejects total non-violence'. He has been awarded several honorary degrees, a life peerage, the Order of Friendship of Russia, a Fellowship of the Royal Society of Literature and many other awards.

- See http://rowanwilliams.archbishopofcanterbury.org for further information.

William Wilberforce (1759-1833): Wilberforce was a life-long advocate for the abolition of the slave trade. He came from a well-to-do family in Hull and graduated from Cambridge before entering Parliament. Wilberforce was an Evangelical Christian who was encouraged in his political endeavours by Methodist founder's John and Charles Wesley, former slave-ship captain John Newton and prime minister, William Pitt the Younger. His position against slavery made him deeply unpopular in some quarters and he constantly came up against the argument that abolishing the trade would greatly endanger the whole British economy. Nevertheless, he campaigned vigorously, year in and year out, with the help of other Christians, Quakers and political allies until support grew. In 1806, slave-trading was abolished in all the British colonies and in 1833 all slaves in the British Empire were emancipated. Wilberforce, the man who had played a huge part in this died shortly after.[61] Reddie [62] makes the point that Wilberforce has not gained the recognition that he deserves and that his name is far less well known than of contemporaries Wellington and Nelson.

- See http://abolition.e2bn.org for further information.

Walter Wink (1935-2012): Wink was an American theologian, author and activist who promoted 'Progressive Christianity' and wrote extensively on the subject of non-violent resistance. He was ordained as a Methodist Minister in 1961 and spent much of his working life lecturing and writing. The idea of power structures was central to his teaching and he also gave workshops in churches and was a Fellow of the U.S. Institute of Peace.

- See Martin in The New York Times: 19/05/2012 (http://mobile.nytimes.com) for further information

John Woolman (1720-1772): Woolman always sought to lead by example. He showed great concern for the welfare of animals and often chose to walk when travelling rather than use coaches which he felt was cruel to the horses. When his bakery business became too profitable he gave it up in case it compromised his integrity and took up tailoring instead. As a result, he was freer to travel from place to place as an itinerant Quaker minister. He criticised other Quakers who did not show respect for other Christian groups or other faiths. Perhaps most importantly, he campaigned tirelessly against the evils of slavery. His persistence convinced many Quakers who ignored their group's testimony against slavery of the errors of their way. He also tried to promote positive links with the Native Americans whose mistreatment he acknowledged. Although a quiet and solitary man, the publication of his journal in 1774 gave an insight into his character.[63]

- See www.quakersintheworld.org for further information.

John Howard Yoder (1927-1997): Yoder was a theologian who also wrote prolifically on the subject of Christian pacifism. Yoder's ideas were shaped by the Mennonite / Anabaptist background he came from. He did relief work in post-World War Two Europe before embarking on his academic career. He taught at Mennonite seminaries and then at Notre Dame University. He argued that the church lost its integrity after it became a state church rather than a persecuted one. He believed the church should lead by peaceful example rather than forcing its ideas on others. He is best known for his Politics of Jesus, published in 1972. Unfortunately, his reputation has been seriously damaged by allegations of sexual impropriety against numerous female students.

- See Yoder: 1994 for further details.

4. Organisations:

The previous section looked at the contribution made by individual Christians to pacifism and peace-making. This section will examine the role played by churches, charities, foundations, fellowships, societies and non-governmental organisations (NGO's) in promoting peace. Historically, very few churches have accepted a pacifist stance wholesale with the exception of Quakers and some Anabaptist groups such as the Mennonites and Amish. Some other groups profiled, such as the Shakers and Doukhobors, are included to demonstrate the scope of Christian pacifism historically.

Since the twentieth century, many peace initiatives have developed within mainstream denominations and these denominations have often become more open to participating in ecumenism, interfaith dialogue and organisations such as the World Council of Churches, part of whose remit includes the promotion of unity. Many denominations have their own pacifist or peace fellowships or peace and justice networks. Some interfaith organisations, such as Religions for Peace, are included due to the high level of Christian participation in them. Some Christian buildings, such as Coventry Cathedral and St. Ethelburga's Centre for Reconciliation and Peace in London, feature because of their dedication to the promotion of peace and unity. Due to the range of groups and institutions on offer, no Christian has an excuse for being unable to engage with peace issues. I quote frequently, and sometimes extensively, from the featured organisation's websites as their own words often best describe their aims but I also keep an eye on the views that outsiders have of those organisations. The diversity of approaches helps to dispel the myth that Christians are either harmless do-gooders or trouble-makers. Profiled organisations often have vast experience in collaborating, networking, capacity-building, dialoguing, mediating, reconciling, protesting, accompanying, lobbying, advocating, training and educating.

Anglican Peace and Justice Network (APJN): The Anglican Peace and Justice Network 'connects Anglicans around the world who share a passion for conflict resolution, peace-building, and seeking Christ-centred justice for all people'. They aim to highlight justice and peace issues within the Anglican communion, to promote the rights of marginalised people, to support the work done by Anglicans worldwide for peace and to educate and advocate for global reconciliation.

• See www.apjn.anglican.communion.org for further information.

Anglican Pacifist Fellowship (APF): Although many denominations have peace fellowships, Anglicans have a pacifist fellowship implying a rejection of all violence rather than just the promotion of peace initiatives. It was founded in 1937 by Anglican clergyman Dick Sheppard to counteract support in some quarters of the Church of England for the looming war with Germany. Its membership came to include not just clergymen, but lay people such as ex-Labour leader George Lansbury and writers Vera Brittain and Evelyn Underhill. Brittain's writings were highly critical of saturation aerial bombing of cities and civilian areas. The Anglican Pacifist Fellowship provided support to conscientious objectors during the Second World War, facilitating social projects as an alternative to armed service. Canon John Collins, a Fellowship member, was involved in the founding of the Campaign for Nuclear Disarmament (CND). The Fellowship was also instrumental in shifting the Anglican church as a whole towards a more peaceful stance. The rights of conscientious objectors were recognised and supported by the 1968 Lambeth Conference. The Anglican Pacifist

Fellowship believes that war is incompatible with the teaching of Jesus, that churches should never support war and that Christian should oppose the waging or justification of war. They pray for and actively work for peace through education and supporting others in opposing violence. It is vital that the Anglican Communion has this pacifist wing due to the powerful Constantinian relationship between the British Government and the Church of England. Bruce Kent [1] claims that Harold Wilson secretly tried to sway some of the Anglican bishops into opposing CND. It is important to have a group within the established church to counter misinformation.

- See www.anglicanpeacemaker.org.uk for further information.

The Anabaptist Network: The Anabaptist Network is a network of individuals in the UK who are interested in learning more about the Anabaptist tradition and how Anabaptist ideas have influenced not just Anabaptist groups such as Mennonites but also the wider church. Its following is inter-denominational and dialogue is encouraged to promote Anabaptist ideas including the need for peace. This is summed up on the website stating that 'peace is at the heart of the Gospels' and that individuals holding Anabaptist convictions 'are committed to finding non-violent alternatives and to learning how to make peace between individuals, within and among churches, in society and between nations.' Along with the Mennonite Trust, the Anabaptist Network also supports the work of the Centre for Anabaptist Studies in Bristol Baptist College to promote the study of Anabaptist history and theology.

- See www.anabaptistnetwork.com for further information.

The Archbishop Romero Trust: The Archbishop Romero Trust seeks not just to highlight the life and work of the El Salvadoran Archbishop who was assassinated for speaking out against the injustices in his country but also to 'provide support to human rights and social justice initiatives in Latin America which carry forward the tradition of his work'. The patrons of the trust include not only Catholics, but prominent Anglicans, such as the Archbishop of York John Sentamu and ex-Archbishop of Canterbury Rowan Williams, reflecting the strong cross-denominational interest in Romero's life and legacy.

- See www.romerotrust.org.uk for further information.

Baptist Peace Fellowship: The Baptist Peace Fellowship aims to unite Baptists who find the use of force incompatible with the teachings of Jesus. They are committed to working with others who seek to use non-violence to overcome injustice and to promote peace in national, community and personal life. They aim to achieve their goals through publication of peace materials, giving talks in churches, attending peace demonstrations, lobbying M.P.s and through working with other peace groups.

- See www.baptist-peace.org.uk for further information.

Bruderhof: Bruderhof communities were founded in Germany in 1920 by a theology teacher named Eberhard Arnold who was inspired by the Hutterian Anabaptist tradition. They were intended to allow members to live a simple life and at the same time to promote peace and harmony.[2] There are communities in Australia, Germany, Paraguay, the United Kingdom and the United States. They practice adult baptism and state that because 'our faith transcends political and nationalistic affiliations', that 'we are also pacifists and conscientious objectors'. About 2,700 individuals live in Bruderhof communities worldwide and communities include single persons, couples and children, who, in imitation of the early church, share everything in common.

- See www.bruderhof.com for further information.

CAFOD: The Catholic Agency for Oversees Development is 'the official aid agency of the Catholic Church in England and Wales'. They work with people from all backgrounds globally to tackle poverty and injustice. They cite scriptures along with Catholic Social Teaching as the inspiration for their work. As part of the Caritas Internationalis network, they are well placed to work in partnership with other Caritas branches throughout the world, as well as local churches in those areas, to deliver aid and to campaign against injustice. They are also committed to inspiring young people to get involved in campaigns for development and justice and to try and build a more secure and peaceful world.

- See www.cafod.org.uk for further information.

Caritas Internationalis: Caritas Internationalis is a development charity which 'shares the mission of the Catholic church to serve the poor and promote charity and justice throughout the world'. They advocate responding compassionately and practically to events which affect the poor and marginalised globally such as conflict, natural disasters and climate change. They call on Catholics worldwide to enlist the Gospel values to tackle poverty and violence. The history of Caritas goes back to 1897, when the first Caritas was founded in Germany and subsequently other branches emerged throughout Europe and America before expanding globally from the nineteen sixties onwards. It is perceived as an official Church agency existing to provide poverty relief in a global context. It has been active in some of the areas hit hardest by poverty and conflict including India, Pakistan, Vietnam, the Middle East, Cambodia, El Salvador, Ethiopia, Rwanda and Eastern Europe. It has adapted to respond to new challenges such as climate change, human trafficking and Western homelessness and in 2010, Pope Benedict visited a Caritas homeless shelter in Rome. It also acts to tackle the causes of injustice, such as through support the adaptation of Convention 189 by the International Labour Organisation to protect vulnerable domestic workers. In 2012 its status as an official church agency was reaffirmed when the Vatican approved New Statutes and Rules for Caritas. The ongoing crisis in Syria and the surrounding area continues to be a major focus of attention for Caritas efforts currently. They are keen to ensure that they work with anyone who is poor and vulnerable irrespective of religion or ethnicity.

- See www.caritas.org for more information.

Carter Centre: The Carter Centre was founded by ex-U.S. President Jimmy Carter and he was awarded the Nobel Peace Prize for its achievements. The Carter Centre is 'guided by a fundamental commitment to human rights and the alleviation of human suffering' and 'seeks to prevent and resolve conflicts, enhance freedom and democracy, and improve health'. It promotes the use of evidence-based practice in its interventions and seeks to work in partnership with other organisations, local communities and governments who share its aims. Although not a specifically Christian organisation, the Carter Center reflects its founder's Christian commitment to peace and justice.

- See www.cartercenter.org for more information.

Catholic Worker Movement: The Catholic Worker is a movement that is 'ecumenical, pacifist and anarchist in the spirit of gentle personalism.' It is an international movement whose individual communities are based on 'works of mercy' such as tackling poverty, working with the homeless and visiting those in prison. The Catholic Worker Movement was founded in 1933 in the middle of the

American Depression by Dorothy Day and Peter Maurin who aimed to put Catholic Social Teaching into action in the service of the poor and marginalised and to tackle the injustice and poverty that leads to violence. The movement runs 'houses of hospitality' that are intended to be centres of community and temporary shelters for those in need. Houses of hospitality are run by volunteers dedicated to service to others. Resistance to injustice and violence is seen as an integral part of this work. They also engage in actions which are more overtly political such as protesting against nuclear weapons.

- See www.catholicworker.org for further information.

Centre for Action and Contemplation: The Centre for Action and Contemplation was founded by the Franciscan priest and author Richard Rohr in New Mexico in 1986 to attempt to integrate the way of contemplation and action. They seek to be 'a centre for experiential education, rooted in the Gospels, encouraging the transformation of human consciousness through contemplation, and equipping people to be instruments of peaceful change in the world'. They seek to harness people's deeper spiritual intuitions to 'encourage actions for justice rooted in prayer'. They work in co-operation with individuals from other religions and cultures.

- See www.cac.org for further information.

Christian Aid: Although Christian Aid is not specifically a peace organisation, its website states that they aim to combat poverty worldwide and to work for social justice for the marginalised, both of which are key elements in the search for global peace. In certain instances they participate in specific peace initiatives such as in Sudan where they work with the South Sudan Council of Churches to advocate for peace through dialogue and reconciliation. They seek to work in partnership not just with churches, but also other faith groups and secular organisations with similar aims. Their values include love, solidarity, dignity, respect, justice, equality, co-operation and partnership all of which contribute to a more peaceful and harmonious world.

- See www.christianaid.org.uk for further information.

Christians Aware: Christians Aware is 'an international and interdenominational educational charity working to develop multicultural and interfaith understanding and friendship locally, nationally and internationally' and its aim 'is to work for justice, peace and development' with a focus on 'listening to encourage awareness and action.' Christians Aware have a number of aims including promoting interfaith education, encouraging international visits and exchanges, undertaking justice and peace work and producing and distributing educational materials. Christians Aware are based in Leicester and maintain strong links with other religious groups in this multi-faith city.

- See www.christiansaware.co.uk for more information.

Christian Campaign for Nuclear Disarmament: Christian CND's website states 'Christian CND is a specialist section of the Campaign for Nuclear Disarmament. Christian CND provides a focus for Christians who want to witness on the basis of their faith against nuclear weapons and other weapons of mass destruction, while also positively campaigning for peace.' They are firmly opposed to Trident, Britain's submarine-based nuclear arsenal, which consists of four submarines, each carrying 48 warheads several times the strength of the Hiroshima bomb, which cost the U.K. tens of billions of pounds to maintain. Christian CND publishes a regular magazine called 'Ploughshare'.

- See www.christiancnd.org.uk for further information.

Christian Peacemaker Teams (CPT): Christian Peacemaker Teams are spiritually rooted in Mennonite, Quaker and Brethren principles but look to 'the whole church' to transform an often violent world through non-violence, action and working in partnership with local peace activists. They perceive violence, conflict and war to be rooted in injustice and 'systemic structures of oppression'. They reinforce a peaceful approach through a broad ecumenical network enlisting the help of others from different denominational perspectives. This provides a unified Christian response to the issues they are engaging with. The CPT approach encourages 'spiritually-centred peacemaking, creative public witness, non-violent direct action and protection of human rights'. CPT emerged among the Peace Churches in the 1980's as a response to some in those churches who wanted to put their faith into practice through non-violent action in solidarity with those in conflict zones globally. Teams set up projects in areas as diverse as Haiti, Mexico and the West Bank. Initially sponsorship came from North American Mennonites and Brethren, but later other denominations such as Baptists and Presbyterians made contributions. The nature of the work undertaken changes in response to the challenges presented and today CPT are involved in Columbia, Kurdistan, Palestine, the US 'Borderlands' and Africa. They also provide specialist training in non-violent approaches to resolving conflict.

- See www.cpt.org for more information.

Community of Sant'Egidio: The Community of Sant'Egidio began life in Rome in 1968 as a Catholic lay community and now has more than 60,000 members globally. Sant'Egidio, founded by Andrea Riccardi, started as a small group trying to put the Gospels into action by visiting and assisting the poor and marginalised living in the shanty towns on the outskirts of Rome. They started small informal schools there which subsequently grew into 'schools of peace'. The different worldwide branches of the community are united by a common spirituality and a commitment to prayer, charity, ecumenism, solidarity with the poor and dialogue as a way of promoting co-operation and peace between religions and as a means of resolving conflict and promoting reconciliation. They are engaged in opposing the death penalty, promoting ecumenism and interfaith dialogue as well as working tirelessly for peace. They have been active promoting dialogue between the Catholic and Orthodox branches of Christianity and also view interfaith dialogue as a key component in the fostering of harmony. They believe that conflict and poverty go hand and hand in the destruction of civil society and that justice must be promoted in order to bring lasting peace. They have earned a reputation for being effective peace builders and reconcilers and have played an important mediatory role in resolving conflicts in Mozambique and the Balkans. They have earned much recognition for this work including the World Methodist Peace Award, the Niwano Peace Prize, the Balzan Prize and the International Charlemagne Prize.

- See www.santegidio.org for more information.

Council of Christians and Jews (CCJ): Of all the world religions, it is the Jewish one, perhaps, that Christians most need to ensure good relations with. From the time of the early church contact between these two faiths has been strained. This relationship deteriorated significantly from the late Middle Ages onwards leading to massacres and expulsions of Jews in locations as diverse as England, Spain, Portugal and Russia. This was church / state complicity at its worst resulting in a diminished cultural and intellectual life in these areas. As a consequence, Christians need to take some of the responsibility for the ensuing Holocaust in the twentieth century, even if this was instigated by a secular state. Since World War Two great efforts have been made to build bridges between the two faiths. However, there is still much residual anti-Semitism in some left-wing, right-wing and academic circles.

The Council of Christians and Jews (CCJ) was founded in Britain in 1942, at the height of World War Two, by Chief Rabbi Joseph H. Hertz and Archbishop William Temple to promote mutual understanding between the two faiths. Queen Elisabeth the Second is its patron. The aims of the CCJ are 'celebrating the history and diversity of both communities, facilitating constructive dialogue, enabling meaningful learning experiences and providing opportunities for transformative change.' It aims to facilitate change through education, dialogue and social action. Its work is especially important in these volatile political times when incidences of anti-Semitism are not uncommon in Britain and Europe.

- See www.ccj.org.uk for further information.

Coventry Cathedral: Coventry Cathedral's history has led to it developing a unique ministry of reconciliation. The original medieval cathedral was destroyed during a devastating night of bombing in 1940 during the Blitz. On Christmas day of the same year, Provost Dick Howard vowed on radio that in the aftermath of the war he would work with those who were now perceived as the enemy to promote reconciliation and peace. The medieval ruins are designated as a memorial to civilian casualties of war and are used to draw attention to the issues of aerial bombing, sexual violence in war zones, the plight of refugees, environmental damage in areas of conflict, the use of child soldiers and the dangers of landmines. The Coventry Cathedral Medieval Ruins project seeks to raise awareness of the devastation of conflict through art, education, prayer and worship. After the destruction of the cathedral, three medieval nails were fashioned into the shape of a cross and the 'Cross of Nails' became a potent symbol for hope and friendship in the post-World War Two world. Similar crosses were presented, as a sign of friendship, to German cities such as Berlin and Dresden. The Community of the Cross of Nails now has over 200 partners in 35 countries worldwide working together to promote reconciliation.

- See www.coventrycathedral.org for more information.

The Doukhobors: The Doukhobors were a Christian group that originated in Tsarist Russia and who were persecuted due to their pacifism and rejection of the Russian government brutality and the monopoly of the Orthodox church. Because of this persecution, many of them emigrated to Canada at the start of the twentieth century helped financially and on a practical level by supporters of Tolstoy and by Quakers. Before this, many had faced internal exile in Central Asia. Tolstoy used the earnings from his novel Resurrection to help finance the passage of Doukhobars to Canada.[3] There may be up to 40,000 Doukhobors descendants in Canada today, but only a fraction of these acknowledge their religious heritage.

- See www.uscdoukhobors.org for further information.

Ecumenical Accompaniment Programme in Palestine and Israel (EAPPI): The Ecumenical Accompaniment Programme in Palestine and Israel state they offer a 'vision of justice and peace in Palestine and Israel' that 'brings international human rights monitors to witness life under occupation and go home to promote change'. The programme is coordinated by the World Council of Churches acting in response to pleas by Palestinian Christians for help from the outside. The scheme was instigated in 2002, and since then several hundred volunteers have participated, volunteering for three months at a time. They aim to contribute towards an eventual resolution of the conflict through witnessing to life under occupation, liaising with Palestinians and Israelis who are working towards peace and through educating others regarding the complexities of the situation. Their presence within vulnerable Palestinian communities there serves to protect them from human rights abuses. They seek to promote co-operation, to be inclusive, impartial and non-violent and to promote a just peace. EAPPI in the British Isles is administered by Quakers in Britain.

- See www.eappi.org for more information.

Elijah Interfaith Institute: The Elijah Interfaith Institute seeks to 'create understanding and harmony between the worlds religions' through 'interfaith dialogue, research and dissemination between the worlds diverse communities'. They aim to bring together religious leaders and scholars from diverse traditions in order to achieve this. Obviously this is not a Christian group but Christians rightly participate in its activities which go to foster good relations between various faith communities. It is important that Christian peace makers avail of every opportunity to engage with those around them and institutions such as the Elijah Institute are vital to this process. Elijah is a prophet recognised by Judaism, Christianity and Islam and serves as a spiritual link between these faiths. Some prominent Christian scholars such as Hans Kung and Marcus Braybrooke have contributed to the work of the Elijah Institute. Also, the Elijah Institute is based in Jerusalem, a city sacred to the monotheistic religions and a potential symbol of their unity. Yet, too often the city is associated with divisions and conflicts between these faiths. It is imperative that Christian peacemakers contribute to the harmonious development of this beautiful and mystical city and to fostering a genuine peace within its confines.

- See www.elijah-interfaith.org.uk for more information.

Fellowship of Reconciliation: In 1914 pacifists from several Christian denominations met for a conference in Cambridge and founded the Fellowship of Reconciliation. This conference was organised by a Quaker, Harry Hodgkin. Many of those who attended believed that it was impossible to reconcile war with Christianity and that Christians should be committed to the ministry of reconciliation.[4] The Fellowship of Reconciliation has permanent representation at the United Nations. The Fellowship tackles various specific issues such as community conflict transformation projects overseas, non-violent conflict resolution and opposing the use of armed drones. Some of the issues it has been involved with in the past include the opposing the First World War, rescuing Jews from Nazi tyranny, working with Martin Luther King to further Civil Rights, supporting War Resisters International to get conscientious objection enshrined in European nation's law, etc. Six Nobel Laureates were members including Martin Luther King (1964), Jane Adams (1931), Mairead Corrigan (1976), Adolfo Perez Esquivel (1980) and Emily Green Balch (1946).

- See www.for.org for further information.

Habitat for Humanity: Habitat for Humanity is a 'non-profit, ecumenical Christian ministry that builds with people in need regardless of race or religion' and welcomes 'volunteers and supporters from all backgrounds'. They are represented in over 70 countries globally and try to improve people's living conditions by providing basic and affordable housing to people from impoverished backgrounds. They aim to improve housing where people live in slums, have been affected by natural disaster or conflict and warfare. Ex-U.S. President and Nobel Laureate Jimmy Carter was involved in and committed to the work of this organisation and participated in the actual building of homes for them.

- See www.habitat.org for more information.

International Association for Religious Freedom (IARF): The importance of interfaith dialogue to the promotion of peace and harmony globally cannot be over-emphasised. In order to do this effectively, individuals and groups need to be able to articulate their beliefs without fear of discrimination, victimisation or violence. Although not a Christian organisation, the IARF has many Christian members and for more than a century 'has stood for and worked towards cultural and interfaith understanding, justice, peace and religious freedom'. They claim to be the oldest inter-religious organisation and are proud of their 'corporate memberships by religious communities'. They also welcome individual membership from those who share their aims. The IARF have United Nations consultative status and actively promote the principles of the 1981 Declaration on the Elimination of all Forms of Intolerance and Discrimination Based on Religion or Belief (DEIDRB). The IARF is supported in this work by many Christian denominations including the Roman Catholic Church, and in 2010 the Pontifical Council for Justice and Peace sent a letter to the IARF's Congress in Kerala, India reaffirming the Church's commitment to interfaith dialogue. The Unitarians, with their interest in incorporating aspects of different faiths, have always been keen supporters of this organisation and the first secretary of the IARF, Dr. Charles William Wendte, was a Unitarian, and many of its present individual members are Unitarians.[5]

- See www.iarf.net for further information.

Living Stones of the Holy Land Trust: The Living Stones of the Holy Land Trust aims to educate people about the reality and make-up of Christianity in the Holy Land and nearby countries. It was founded by Reverend Michael Prior, an advocate of Palestinian rights, who died in 2004. The trust aims to raise awareness in Britain and further afield about Christians in the Holy Land, to facilitate encounters with Palestinian Christians through pilgrimages, and to work with other groups to promote these aims. It also provides bursaries for Palestinian students to study theology and other subjects at university level. The trust runs a theology group which addresses issues faced by Christians and others affected by conflict in the region and holds lectures on these subjects in Britain. This work is very important as many in the U.K. have little awareness of the diversity and complexity of the Christian community in Jerusalem and the surrounding region. Although the Christian community in the Holy Land numbers only about 150,000 (who are mainly Palestinian), it is made up of many diverse groups including Armenian, Syrian, Ethiopian, Coptic, Greek and Russian Orthodox, Roman, Greek, Melkite, Syrian, Maronite, Armenian, Chaldean and Coptic Catholics, Anglicans, Lutherans and others. Many of these groups have been established in the region since pre-Islamic times, but are now under threat of extinction due to political and economic reasons.

- See www.livingstonesonline.org.uk and Hilliard and Bailey: 1999 for more information.

Mennonites: Mennonites are a group of Christians with Anabaptist origins. At the time of the Reformation Anabaptists went further than other group in rejecting infant baptism. The also rejected state church ties and members were required to be voluntarily baptised as adults. They were persecuted by Catholic and Protestant alike. A former Dutch priest, Menno Simons, managed to unite some divergent

83

Anabaptist groups and his followers became known as Mennonites. From the start Mennonites rejected war and violence and embraced pacifism.[6] There are estimated to be about 1.2 million Mennonites in the world today. Many of them live in Canada and the U.S. but they also have a global presence as well. Mennonites continue to maintain a pacifist perspective, rejecting war and actively endeavouring to be peacebuilders. The strength that peace churches, such as Mennonites, have, is that pacifism is integral to their Christianity and Christianity integral to their pacifism.

- See www.thirdway.com for further information.

The Mennonite Trust: The Mennonite Trust states its aim is to 'serve the wider Christian community by promoting the understanding and practice of Mennonite and other Anabaptist life' and through the 'embodying of Mennonite and other Anabaptist values and spirituality through hospitality, friendship, worship and educational activities.' It works in partnership with the Anabaptist Network to promote Anabaptist values, including peace and reconciliation, as well as supporting Anabaptist education and research through the Centre of Anabaptist Studies based in Bristol Baptist College.

- See www.menno.org for more information.

Methodist Peace Fellowship: The Methodist Peace Fellowship was founded in 1933 to 'inform and unite Methodists who covenanted together to renounce war and all its works and ways' and is affiliated to the Fellowship of Reconciliation. It accepts the basic principles of the Fellowship of Reconciliation and all members of the Methodist Peace Fellowship are also automatically members of the Fellowship of Reconciliation, England.

- See www.mpf.org.uk for more information.

The Molokans: The Molokans were a group of pacifist Christians living on the Russian steppes. Molakans, which means 'milk-drinkers', supposedly got their name because they continued to drink milk on Orthodox fast days when dairy products were generally avoided. Their religious practice consisted mainly of Bible study.[7] They were persecuted by the authorities for their pacifism and lack of compliance and were often exiled to outlying areas such as Armenia, Azerbaijan and Siberia. Tolstoy showed great interest in their beliefs and welfare. Some Molokans emigrated to the U.S. and Mexico in search of a more tolerant environment. Small number of Molokans still live in Russia, Central Asia and North America.

- See https://molokans.wordpress.com for more information.

Moravian Church: The Moravian Church originated in Fifteenth Century Bohemia, stemming from the teachings of John Huss who was burned as a heretic in 1415. His followers became known as the Bohemian Brethren and a group of them who sought refuge from persecution in Saxony in 1722 became known as the Moravian Brethren. They soon became dedicated missionaries to the New World, and elsewhere, and today there are approximately 750,000 members of the church globally. They hold values such as simplicity, fellowship and service to others. They had a formative influence on the theology of John and Charles Wesley who went on to found the Methodist church. The Moravians foster an ecumenical outlook, seek harmony with other Christian groups and endeavour to promote peace.

- See www.moravian.org.uk for more information.

Plowshares Movement: The Plowshares Movement was founded in the U.S. by the Berrigan Brothers, and a number of other Christian pacifists, to provide opposition to nuclear weapons through non-violent direct action. The name is taken from the Book of Isaiah which talks about the beating of swords into plowshares, in other words, converting weapons into something beneficial and productive for society. Their actions have involved entering military premises and symbolically beating weaponry with hammers. Sentences given to those involved are often several years in federal prisons.

The Quakers: The Quakers, or Society of Friends, emerged in the mid-seventeenth century under the leadership of George Fox who brought together a number of distinct groups with similar radical religious ideas. The movement spread quickly and, as it was seen as a threat to the status quo, Quakers were severely persecuted with thousands imprisoned.[8] This did not deter them from being 'publishers of Truth', nor provoke them to violence. The pacifist ideals of the Quakers were spelt out in the 1660 letter to King Charles the Second entitled the 'Harmless and Innocent People of God, called Quakers'.[9] Their compassionate approach led them to promote the abolition of slavery and to advocate penal reform and an enlightened approach towards mental illness. In North America, they mediated between colonials and the Native Americans. The Peace Testimony led to Quakers responding in creative ways to the conflicts of the twentieth century, through the foundation of the Friends Ambulance Unit and the undertaking of relief work which was acknowledged through the awarding of the Nobel Peace Prize in 1947. Quakers have also been highly active in different organisations which promote non-violence such as the Fellowship of Reconciliation.[10] The website of the British Quakers states that 'Quakers believe that there is something of God in everyone' and their faith is lived through action leading to them working 'positively and creatively with others to build a just and more peaceful world.'

The simplicity of the Quaker approach is also summed up in the statement 'We try to live in truth, peace, simplicity and equality, finding God in ourselves and those around us.'

• See www.quaker.org.uk for more information.

Orthodox Peace Fellowship: The full name of the Orthodox Peace Fellowship is the Orthodox Peace Fellowship of the Protection of the Mother of God, indicating the extent to which its principles are directly influenced by Orthodox theology. Members seek to 'practice the Christian peacemaking vocation in every area of life' and to 'bear witness to the peace of Christ by applying the principles of the Gospel to situations of division and conflict at every level of human relationship, and to promote prayer and worship, acts of mercy and service, and love for all human beings and all creation.' They deny any political or ideological affiliation apart from the Christian faith. They promote an acknowledgement that all are equal in the eyes of God, that life should always be respected, that conflict should be resolved through mediation, that injustice should be tackled without resorting to violence and that conscientious objectors should be supported. Although members are not expected to be pacifists, they believe that Orthodox theology does not support Just War Theory and that all non-violent means should be considered in resolving conflicts. They support compassionate treatment of prisoners and restorative justice and reject the use of capital punishment. The Orthodox Peace Fellowship endeavours to achieve its aims through theological research, publication and providing practical assistance in conflict zones.

• See www.incommunion.org for more information.

Pax Christi International: Pax Christi International 'is a global Catholic peace movement working worldwide to establish, peace, respect for human rights, justice and reconciliation.' It was founded in Europe in 1945, in the aftermath of the Second World War, and comprises of dozens of autonomous national sections worldwide. Although a Catholic organisation, it operates independent of church structures but members include lay people, priests and bishops. While mindful of the negative side of religion, the organisation tries to emphasise that which is positive in order to build a more peaceful society. It endeavours to do this by facilitating growth within the movement internationally, assisting member organisations to undertake active peace work and through promoting the spiritual dimension of this work. Pax Christi is well placed to do this as it has it has special consultative status at the United Nations and through its Brussels office is able to develop extensive networks and close relationships with other Non-Governmental Organisations (NGO's). Pax Christi values interfaith and ecumenical dialogue and welcomes the opportunity to work in partnership with groups from other denominations and faiths as well as secular groups who share some of the same aims. They seek to encourage people to work for peace and to acknowledge significant achievements of individuals and organisations in this area through the Pax Christi International Peace Awards. Examples of past winners include French politician Jacques Delors in 2005 for his commitment to European peace and security and the Women's Active Museum on War and Peace in 2006 for its work towards healing women of the effects of wartime sexual violence.

- See www.paxchristi.net for more information.

Pax Christi U.K.: Pax Christi U.K. state they work for peace based on justice, reconciliation on a local and international level and the promotion of non-violence as a way of living. Pax Christi, U.K. place a good deal of emphasis on working with youth and educating them about peace and they endeavour to do this through supporting teachers, chaplains and youth workers in promoting a culture of non-violence.

- See www.paxchristi.org.uk for more information.

Religions for Peace: Religions for Peace is not a specifically Christian organisation but a sizable number of Christians are involved with this project. With a large presence among numerous religions worldwide, it does vital work in 'creating multi-religious partnerships to confront our most dire issues; stopping war, ending poverty, and protecting the earth.' It emphasises the importance in religions dialoguing and collaborating together to tackle these issues. It recognises the importance of religious communities as 'the largest and best-organised civil institutions in the world, claiming the allegiance of billions across race, class and national divides'. They harness the support of individual donors, faith-based organisations, foundations, Non-Governmental Organisations (NGO's) and government agencies to promote development, peace and a sustainable environment. It endeavours to ensure that women and young people are as involved as possible in these projects.

- See www.religionsforpeace.org.uk for more information.

The Shakers: The Shakers originated in eighteenth century England and settled in colonial America where they led a communal and pacifist lifestyle and promoted respect for the role of women, with females holding prominent leadership positions. The famous Shaker furniture they produced reflected the simplicity of their lives. Their worship had an ecstatic quality, leading to them being known as the 'shaking Quakers'. Because of their pacifist beliefs, they cared for both Union and Confederate soldiers during the American Civil War and they gained recognition for their conscientious objection. By the twentieth century, the community was in decline and is, by now, almost extinct.

• See http://maineshakers.com for more information.

The Soul of Europe: The Soul of Europe work 'as catalysts and mediators to ensure a peaceful resolution to conflicts – particularly in the Balkans'. They aim to do this by 'bringing people together to help them begin to take steps towards justice and reconciliation'. Staff include both Christians and Muslims who are expected to be impartial. Donald Reeves, an Anglican clergyman, who founded the organisation identifies four steps in bringing enemies together. These steps are putting yourself in the other's shoes, breaking down walls between communities, resolving conflicts involving land ownership and usage, and getting people around a table to address their differences. They also have run a number of specific projects to promote reconciliation, including projects to reconstruct places of worship belonging to different religious communities in Bosnia, promoting interfaith dialogue and tackling Islamophobia in Europe.

• See www.soulofeurope.org for more information.

St. Ethelburga's Centre for Reconciliation and Peace: Like Coventry Cathedral, St. Ethelburga's story developed through adverse circumstances. Situated in the City of London, this church was built in the mid-Sixteenth Century, survived the Great Fire of London and the Blitz only to be seriously damaged by an IRA bomb in 1993. After nearly a decade of fundraising and work, the re-opened church was designated a centre for reconciliation and peace. The Centre aims to promote peace through dialogue, capacity-building, collaboration, education and developing leadership. St. Ethelburga's still functions as a place of worship with regular services, a resident chaplain and opportunities for meditation. Many believe it is very important for Christian peace organisations to continue to pray, meditate and worship in order to maintain the relationship between faith and peace.

- See www.stethelburgas.org for more information.

St. Philip's Centre: The St. Philip's Centre in Leicester is a charity which promotes interfaith understanding and is 'committed to a wide programme of training, public benefit activities and community engagement' which 'is reflected not only in dialogues between different faiths, so crucial in the process of building understanding, friendship and trust, but also in the active involvement of the Centre in community life'. They encourage Christians to engage with other faiths and try to promote a greater understanding of religions in workplaces and among young people.

- See www.stphilipscentre.co.uk for more information.

Tolstoyan Communities / Colonies: During the latter part of Tolstoy's life, and after his death, followers of his philosophy and religious beliefs founded communities in which to put his ideals into practice. This movement was often Christian, pacifist and vegetarian in orientation with communities in America, Europe and Russia, where the colonies were subjected to severe pressures during the Soviet era and especially during the process of 'collectivisation'. Gandhi named his ashram in South Africa 'Tolstoy Farm', in recognition of the influence that Tolstoy had on his beliefs.

Tutu Foundation: The Tutu Foundation was founded by the dean of Southwark Cathedral, the Very Reverend Colin Slee, along with his wife Edith, with the support of Archbishop Desmond Tutu. Taking the South African concept of Ubuntu which recognises our human interconnectedness as its model, it seeks to resolve conflict through reconciliation. It teaches that if you dehumanize another you dehumanize yourself. Tutu Foundation, UK, uses this model to engage with young people caught up in gang violence and to support the ongoing peace process in Northern Ireland. It seeks to overcome bullying, prejudice and discrimination and also provides specialist mediation services.

- See www.tutufoundationuk.org for more information.

Unitarian Peace Fellowship: The Unitarian Peace Fellowship is one of a number of societies within the Unitarian Church in the UK. It was founded to witness for peace in 1916 at the height of the First World War. It highlights the centrality of compassion in the promotion of peace and reconciliation and encourages Unitarians to promote these values locally, nationally and internationally. Unitarians are also prominent in the related areas of interfaith dialogue and the promotion of religious freedom.

- See www.ukunitarians.org.uk for more information.

Unitarians: The Unitarian movement originated in fifteenth century Poland and Transylvania and had become established in Britain by the late Eighteenth Century. Unitarians are religious liberals who promote the idea of divine unity and the oneness of God. Because of this, they respect those who follow different paths of faith. They promote values such as liberty, integrity, conscience, compassion, justice and peace and they look to spirituality, science and the arts to provide meaning. While Unitarianism arose out of Christianity, and many Unitarians still regard themselves as Christian, the Unitarian tradition incorporates elements of many different faiths and spiritualities. Congregations are independent of each other but are affiliated to the General Assembly of Unitarian and Free Christian Churches in Britain, and to the Unitarian Universalist Association in the U.S. Because of their belief in the Oneness of God, Unitarians are committed to dialoguing with other faiths.

- See www.ukunitarians.org.uk for more information.

United Reformed Peace Fellowship: The United Reformed Peace Fellowship state that they are 'a group of United Reformed Church people who accept God's call to human beings to live in peace and who are committed to discerning and obeying the urgent call of God to pursue Peace with Justice in the world.' Although the United Reformed Church often makes pronouncements on issues such as war, nuclear weapons and the arms trade, the United Reform Peace Fellowship was founded as a separate group to advocate on these issues within the church.

- See www.urc.org.uk for more information.

Waldensians: The Waldensians are named after Peter Waldo, a merchant from Lyons, who lived in the latter half of the twelfth century. After translating the Latin Bible into French and giving away his property to be able to live a more Christian life, he attracted a band of followers who shared his values. Initially supported by Pope Alexander the Third, they were subsequently prohibited from preaching by the Archbishop of Lyons. When this failed to deter them, Pope Lucius the Third condemned them as heretics and they were subjected to severe persecution. Their influence spread to other areas of Europe such as Lombardy, Provence and central Europe. They operated outside Church structures under the leadership of their own priests who preached in the vernacular and they also reinterpreted the sacraments in their own way.[11] Although the persecution did not stop, they became less isolated after the Reformation with the emergence of different groups which shared their values. There are Waldensian communities today in areas such as Piedmont in Italy, Germany and North and South America. They are involved in working with the marginalised, promoting social justice and dialoguing with other religious groups as well as belonging to the World Council of Churches. In 2015, Pope Francis apologised to the Waldensians for the persecution they suffered at the hands of the Catholic authorities.

- See www.waldensians.org for further information.

World Council of Churches: The World Council of Churches 'is a fellowship of churches which confess the Lord Jesus Christ as God and Saviour according to the scriptures, and therefore seek to fulfil together their common calling to the glory of the one God, Father, Son and Holy Spirit.' The World Council of Churches is a broad coalition of churches which seek to overcome divisions and work towards Christian unity. As a result, members value co-operation and dialogue. The organisation operates on many different levels and has numerous goals including engaging 'in Christian service by serving human need, breaking down barriers between people, seeking justice and peace and upholding the integrity of creation.' Member churches include Anglican, Methodist, Baptist, Lutheran, Reformed, independent and Orthodox churches representing over half a billion adherents.

The origins of the World Council of Churches goes back over a hundred years. In 1910, the World Missionary Conference and later the Orthodox Synod of Constantinople suggested a 'fellowship of churches' and this idea came to fruition with the vote to found the World Council of Churches just prior to the Second World War. The organisation actually came into being after the War, in 1948, and its headquarters is based in Geneva, Switzerland. The Roman Catholic Church is not a member but relations with it have greatly improved.

Numerous World Council of Churches initiatives have positive implications for the search for peace. These projects include the Pilgrimage of Justice and Peace initiative which aims to 'renew the true vocation of the Church through collaborative engagement with the most important issues of justice and peace, healing a world filled with injustice and pain', the Care for Creation and Climate Justice initiative which seeks to recognise a 'God of Justice who protects, loves and cares for the most vulnerable among his creatures' and the Promoting Just Peace initiative which 'assists churches and related groups to make progress toward greater unity for peace'. Highlighted by all this, is the fact that Christians are not placing themselves in a very good position to advocate peace and harmonious co-existence if they do not work hard to get on together.

- See www.oikoumene.org for further information.

5. Conclusion:

To say that we live in uncertain times may be a bit of a cliché; we would not be the first to think this. However, it would be true to say that the post-modern era has produced an unprecedented level of individualism and fragmentation. While many talk about shared values, there is no consensus about what those values are. Whatever perspective we hold, we cannot expect everyone else to share all our views. So much more for religious views which developed under very specific circumstances. If we look hard enough, we can see that different religions hold much in common and religions also share many values with wider secular society. Without diluting the essence of our faith, we must try to focus on those elements that link us to those who do not share it. That may mean focusing on the elements that promote service to others, social justice and peace. If our faith is perceived as a cause of division, it will be limited in the positive effect it has. Unfortunately, there are individuals within all the major faiths who create ammunition for others to use against them. These include fundamentalists or churchmen who are over-bureaucratic and rigid in their approach.

The way to overcome these problems is through dialogue: dialogue between different elements within a denomination, dialogue between different denominations, dialogue between different faiths and dialogue with a wider secular culture. The purpose of this dialogue should not be to dampen down diversity but rather to understand, appreciate and respect it and to pull out elements that are shared to encourage co-operation and friendship. Of course, this is easier said than done and usually only happens in a fragmented way. Globalisation and improved travel and communications present us with endless opportunities to either dialogue with others or to clash with them. Even within the Christian family alone there is so much opportunity for this to happen. Christians hold a whole range of different theologies, practices and viewpoints. A liberal Christian may hold more values in common with secular society than with some other Christians. An individual Christian would find it difficult to define Christianity for others as they would be presenting their version of it. Ecumenical dialogue is vital in order to identify which elements of the faith are common to the different denominations. Of course, there are always groups who will not have any dealings with others but these groups lack the maturity to earn the respect of others.

The mere act of dialoguing with others who you differ with is often a form of peacemaking. Although many Christian groups share certain values, such as charity, making peacemaking a priority would be beneficial in that it reinforces whatever dialogue there is, and also helps present a unified front to the outside world. Faiths that appear to give priority to non-violence or peacemaking, such as the Baha'i, Jain or Buddhist religions, tend to win respect from outsiders, even if those individuals know little else about these traditions. Due to the Quakers emphasis on upholding their peace testimony, people seldom speak as negatively about them, as they sometimes do about some other denominations.

It would be great if Christians were able to say: 'Yes, we have many different groups and values, but we try to talk to each other and not to argue among ourselves; we oppose all wars and promote non-violence and peace as a common standard'. This would give out the message that whatever beliefs are held should only be promoted in a non-violent way and with all due respect for others. Gandhi managed to promote his beliefs among tens of millions. Some have questioned the rightness of those views but no-one can criticise the way he promoted them because he did this non-violently. The same goes for

Martin Luther King and Desmond Tutu and many others. Their genius was not in what they advocated but how they advocated it.

To advocate peace is to disconnect with power and corruption. It is acknowledging that something is not going to work unless people are peaceably won over to it. Christianity is not immediately recognised for its peacemaking, or pacifism, but there are precedents. The life of Jesus and the apostles give an example of a non-violent way forward. The early church was lacking in temporal power and early Christians rejected military service. For many centuries, the Church was so closely tied to the state that it was difficult to identify pacifist elements within it, although there were always individuals who tried to lead peaceful lives. Later, groups with pacifistic leanings emerged such as the Waldenesians, Quakers and Anabaptists. From the 20th Century onwards, individuals within mainstream denominations became more involved in peace work or self-identified as pacifists and many Christian peace groups emerged. In more recent times, interfaith dialogue has developed in momentum and this has provided opportunities to iron out misunderstandings between faith groups that may potentially add to conflict. We live in volatile times, but also times of opportunity if wisdom is exercised. Global Christianity is metamorphosing and needs to develop a positive focus in order to have anything of value to contribute to the world. Due to its universal nature, Christianity has a strong presence in most countries worldwide and, as a result, is in a unique position to be of great benefit if it works positively with others. It needs to be at peace with itself but also to dialogue with and be at peace with others.

Notes:

Chapter 1: History

1. Cato, J. (Introduction): *Mysticism – The Experience of the Divine*: Chronicle books: San Francisco: 1994

2. Starr, M: *God of Love – A Guide to the Heart of Judaism, Christianity and Islam*: Monkfish Book Publishing Company: New York: 2012

3. Gascoigne, B: The Christians: Granada Publishing: London: 1977: p27

4. Holt, B.P.: *A Brief History of Christian Spirituality*: Lion Publishing plc: Oxford: 1997: p27

5. Krieder, A & Yoder, J.H.: *Christians and War* in *The History of Christianity*: Lion Publishing plc: Oxford: 1977: p52

6. Cunningham, M: *Faith in the Byzantine World*: Lion Publishing plc: Oxford: 2002: p71

7. Williams, R: *Where God Happens – Discovering Christ in One Another*: New Seeds: Boston: 2005

8. Clark, K: *The Orthodox Church*: Simple Guides: London: 2009: p155

9. Krieder, A & Yoder, J.H.: *Christians and War* in *The History of Christianity*: Lion Publishing plc: Oxford: 1977: p51

10. Krieder, A & Yoder, J.H.: *Christians and War* in *The History of Christianity*: Lion Publishing plc: Oxford: 1977: p52

11. Markus, G (Ed.): *The Radical Tradition – Saints in the Struggle for Justice and Peace*: Darton, Longman and Todd: London: 1992: pxiii

12. Linder, R.D.: *The Catholic Reformation* in *The History of Christianity*: Lion Publishing plc: Oxford: 1977: p426

13. Sellars, I.: *The Unitarians* in *The History of Christianity*: Lion Publishing plc: Oxford: 1977: p504

14. Chryssides, G.: *The Elements of Unitarianism*: Element Books Ltd: Dorset: 1998: p68

15. Holt, B.P.: *A Brief History of Christian Spirituality*: Lion Publishing plc: Oxford: 1997: p83-88

16. Holt, B.P.: *A Brief History of Christian Spirituality*: Lion Publishing plc: Oxford: 1997: p96

17. Hart, D.B.: *The Story of Christianity – A History of 2000 Years of the Christian Faith*: Quercus: London: 2013: p268

18. Krieder, A & Yoder, J.H.: *The Anabaptists* in *The History of Christianity*: Lion Publishing plc: Oxford: 1977: p404

19. Holt, B.P.: *A Brief History of Christian Spirituality*: Lion Publishing plc: Oxford: 1997: p108

20. Roberts, A.O.: *George Fox and the Quakers* in *The History of Christianity*: Lion Publishing plc: Oxford: 1977: p502

21. Dandelion, P.: *The Quakers – A Short Introduction*: Oxford University Press: Oxford: 2008: p11

22. Alexander, H.G.: *The Growth of the Peace Testimony of the Society of Friends*: Quaker Peace and Service: London: 1982: p3

23. Alexander, H.G.: *The Growth of the Peace Testimony of the Society of Friends*: Quaker Peace and Service: London: 1982: p3-4

24. Holt, B.P.: *A Brief History of Christian Spirituality*: Lion Publishing plc: Oxford: 1997: p110

25. Chryssides, G.: *The Elements of Unitarianism*: Element Books Ltd: Dorset: 1998: p70

26. Chryssides, G.: *The Elements of Unitarianism*: Element Books Ltd: Dorset: 1998: p97

27. Sharma, A.: *Gandhi – A Spiritual Biography*: Yale University Press: 2013: p47

28. Chryssides, G.: *The Elements of Unitarianism*: Element Books Ltd: Dorset: 1998: p73

29. Yogananda, P.: *Autobiography of a Yogi*: Self-Realisation Fellowship: Los Angeles: 2010: p389

30. Bushrui, S. & Jenkins, J.: *Kahlil Gibran, Man and Poet*: Oneworld: Oxford: 2008: p253

31. Kent, B.: *Building the Global Village*: Fount Paperbacks: London: 1991: p59-60

32. Allen, D.: *Mahatma Gandhi*: Reaktion Books Ltd.: London: 2011: p47

33. Allen, D.: *Mahatma Gandhi*: Reaktion Books Ltd.: London: 2011: p44

34. Alexander, H.G.: *The Growth of the Peace Testimony of the Society of Friends*: Quaker Peace and Service: London: 1982: p16

35. Alexander, H.G.: *The Growth of the Peace Testimony of the Society of Friends*: Quaker Peace and Service: London: 1982: p17

36. Alexander, H.G.: *The Growth of the Peace Testimony of the Society of Friends*: Quaker Peace and Service: London: 1982: p17

37. Alexander, H.G.: *The Growth of the Peace Testimony of the Society of Friends*: Quaker Peace and Service: London: 1982: p19

38. Krieder, A & Yoder, J.H.: *Christians and War* in *The History of Christianity*: Lion Publishing plc: Oxford: 1977: p54

Chapter 2: Methods

1. Gascoigne, B: The Christians: Granada Publishing: London: 1977: p271

2. Alexander, H.G.: *The Growth of the Peace Testimony of the Society of Friends*: Quaker Peace and Service: London: 1982: p19

3. Ellsberg, R.: *All Saints – Daily Reflections on Saints, Prophets, and Witnesses of our Time*: The Crossword Publishing Company: New York: 2000: p341

4. Dandelion, P.: *The Quakers – A Short Introduction*: Oxford University Press: Oxford: 2008: p14

5. Alexander, H.G.: *The Growth of the Peace Testimony of the Society of Friends*: Quaker Peace and Service: London: 1982: p27

6. Forest, J.: *Living with Wisdom – A Life of Thomas Merton*: Orbis Books: Maryknoll NY: 1991: p50

7. Forest, J.: *Living with Wisdom – A Life of Thomas Merton*: Orbis Books: Maryknoll NY: 1991: p50

8. Cato, J. (Introduction): *Mysticism – The Experience of the Divine*: Chronicle books: San Francisco: 1994; p40-42

9. Gascoigne, B: The Christians: Granada Publishing: London: 1977: p199-205

10. Gascoigne, B: The Christians: Granada Publishing: London: 1977: p293

Chapter 3: People

1. Dear, J.: *Transfiguration – A Meditation on Transforming Ourselves and Our World*: Doubleday: New York: 2007: p7

2. Kavanagh, J.: *The World is Our Cloister – A Guide to the Modern Religious Life*: O Books: Winchester, 2007: p164

3. Chryssavgis, J. and Gallaher, B.: *Orthodox Meet in Crete* in *The Tablet*: London: 23rd June, 2016

4. Forest, J.: *Living with Wisdom – A Life of Thomas Merton*: Orbis Books: Maryknoll NY: 1991: p50

5. Starr, M: *God of Love – A Guide to the Heart of Judaism, Christianity and Islam*: Monkfish Book Publishing Company: New York: 2012: p126

6. Kent, B.: *Building the Global Village*: Fount Paperbacks: London: 1991: p56-57

7. Alexander, H.G.: *The Growth of the Peace Testimony of the Society of Friends*: Quaker Peace and Service: London: 1982: p27

8. Ellsberg, R.: *All Saints – Daily Reflections on Saints, Prophets, and Witnesses of our Time*: The Crossword Publishing Company: New York: 2000: p519-521

9. Dear, J.: *Transfiguration – A Meditation on Transforming Ourselves and Our World*: Doubleday: New York: 2007: p7

10. Dear, J.: *Transfiguration – A Meditation on Transforming Ourselves and Our World*: Doubleday: New York: 2007: p21-22

11. Forest, J.: Postscript to Hanh, T.N.: *The Miracle of Mindfulness*: Rider: London: 2008: p101

12. Forest, J.: *Living with Wisdom – A Life of Thomas Merton*: Orbis Books: Maryknoll NY: 1991

13. Ellsberg, R.: *All Saints – Daily Reflections on Saints, Prophets, and Witnesses of our Time*: The Crossword Publishing Company: New York: 2000: p27

14. MacCulloch, D.: *Silence – A Christian History*: Penguin Books: London: 2013: p147

15. Ellsberg, R.: *All Saints – Daily Reflections on Saints, Prophets, and Witnesses of our Time*: The Crossword Publishing Company: New York: 2000: p433

16. Ellsberg, R.: *All Saints – Daily Reflections on Saints, Prophets, and Witnesses of our Time*: The Crossword Publishing Company: New York: 2000: p446

17. Durham, G.: *The Spirit of the Quakers*: Yale University Press: New Haven & London: 2010: p83

18. Carson, C. (Ed.): *The Autobiography of Martin Luther King, Jr.*: Grand Central Publishing: NY and Boston: 1998: p24

19. Gandhi, M.K.: *M.K. Gandhi - An Autobiography* or *The Story of my Experiments with Truth*: Penguin: London: 2001: p122-124

20. Shirer, W.L.: *Gandhi – A Memoir: Abacus*: London: 1979: p241

21. Gandhi, M.K.: *M.K. Gandhi - An Autobiography* or *The Story of my Experiments with Truth*: Penguin: London: 2001: p155

22. Allen, D.: *Mahatma Gandhi*: Reaktion Books Ltd.: London: 2011: p43

23. Bushrui, S.: Introduction to Gibran, K.: The Prophet – A New Annotated Edition: Oneworld: London: 201

24. Waterfield, R.: *Kahlil Gibran – Poet of the Soul* in Kumar, S. & Whitefield, F.: Visionaries of the 20th Century – A Resurgence Anthology: Green Books Ltd.: Totnes: 2006: p211

25. Griffiths, B.: *The Golden string – An Autobiography*: Fount Paperbacks: London: 1979: p4

26. Ellsberg, R.: *All Saints – Daily Reflections on Saints, Prophets, and Witnesses of our Time*: The Crossword Publishing Company: New York: 2000: p549

27. Du Boulay, S.: *Bede Griffiths – Modern Mystic* in Kumar, S. & Whitefield, F. (eds.): *Visionaries of the 20th Century – A Resurgence Anthology*: Green Books Ltd.: Totnes: 2006: p191

28. Ellsberg, R.: *All Saints – Daily Reflections on Saints, Prophets, and Witnesses of our Time*: The Crossword Publishing Company: New York: 2000: p550

29. Du Boulay, S.: *Bede Griffiths – Modern Mystic* in Kumar, S. & Whitefield, F. (eds.): *Visionaries of the 20th Century – A Resurgence Anthology*: Green Books Ltd.: Totnes: 2006: p190

30. Du Boulay, S.: *Bede Griffiths – Modern Mystic* in Kumar, S. & Whitefield, F. (eds.): *Visionaries of the 20ᵗʰ Century – A Resurgence Anthology*: Green Books Ltd.: Totnes: 2006: p191

31. Ellsberg, R.: *All Saints – Daily Reflections on Saints, Prophets, and Witnesses of our Time*: The Crossword Publishing Company: New York: 2000: p407-409

32. Ellsberg, R.: *All Saints – Daily Reflections on Saints, Prophets, and Witnesses of our Time*: The Crossword Publishing Company: New York: 2000: p315

33. Ellsberg, R.: *All Saints – Daily Reflections on Saints, Prophets, and Witnesses of our Time*: The Crossword Publishing Company: New York: 2000: p352-353

34. Ellsberg, R.: *All Saints – Daily Reflections on Saints, Prophets, and Witnesses of our Time*: The Crossword Publishing Company: New York: 2000: p341

35. Kent, B.: *Undiscovered Ends – An Autobiography*: Harper Collins: London: 1992: p89

36. Kent, B.: *Building the Global Village*: Fount Paperbacks: London: 1991: p24-27

37. McKitterick, D.: Cardinal Kim Sou-hwan – The First Korean Cardinal and a Campaigner for Human Rights in The Independent: Saturday 21ˢᵗ February 2009

38. Kirk, J.A.: *Martin Luther King* in Kumar. S. & Whitefield, F.: *Visionaries of the 20ᵗʰ Century – A Resurgence Anthology*: Totnes: 2006: p93

39. Carson, C. (Ed.): *The Autobiography of Martin Luther King, Jr.*: Grand Central Publishing: NY and Boston: 1998: p351

40. Kung, H.: *Tracing the Way – Spiritual Dimensions of the World's Religions*: Continuum: London: 2002

41. Butler, B.: *Living with Faith – Journeys towards Trust, Friendship and Justice*: Inspire: Peterborough: 2006

42. Butler, B.: *Living with Faith – Journeys towards Trust, Friendship and Justice*: Inspire: Peterborough: 2006: p116

43. Ellsberg, R.: *All Saints – Daily Reflections on Saints, Prophets, and Witnesses of our Time*: The Crossword Publishing Company: New York: 2000: p203

44. Ellsberg, R.: *All Saints – Daily Reflections on Saints, Prophets, and Witnesses of our Time*: The Crossword Publishing Company: New York: 2000: p538

45. Meddler, L.: *Thomas Merton – Activist Monk* in Kumar, S. & Whitefield, F. (eds.): *Visionaries of the 20th Century – A Resurgence Anthology*: Green Books: Totnes: 2006: p195

46. Forest, J.: *Living with Wisdom – A Life of Thomas Merton*: Orbis Books: Maryknoll NY: 1991: p191

47. Ellsberg, R.: *All Saints – Daily Reflections on Saints, Prophets, and Witnesses of our Time*: The Crossword Publishing Company: New York: 2000: p410-412

48. Dear, J.: *Henri Nouwen's Spirituality of Peace* in *National Catholic Recorder*: Kansas: Oct. 17, 2006

49. Ellsberg, R.: *All Saints – Daily Reflections on Saints, Prophets, and Witnesses of our Time*: The Crossword Publishing Company: New York: 2000: p184

50. Walker, D.: *A Dangerous Priest* in *Church of England Newspaper*: London: 13/02/2012

51. Ellsberg, R.: *All Saints – Daily Reflections on Saints, Prophets, and Witnesses of our Time*: The Crossword Publishing Company: New York: 2000: p132

52. Brabazon, J.: *Albert Schweitzer – Reverence for Life* in Kumar, S. & Whitefield, F. (eds.): *Visionaries of the 20th Century – A Resurgence Anthology*: Green Books, Ltd.: Totnes: 2006: p153

53. Holt, B.P.: *A Brief History of Christian Spirituality*: Lion Publishing plc: Oxford: 1997: p96

54. Peel, M.: *The Last Wesleyan – A Life of Donald Soper*: The Cromwell Press: Wiltshire: 2008

55. Muggeridge, M.: *Conversion*: Hodder & Stoughton: London: 1996: p158

56. Ellsberg, R.: *All Saints – Daily Reflections on Saints, Prophets, and Witnesses of our Time*: The Crossword Publishing Company: New York: 2000: p506

57. Schumacher, D.: *Desmond Tutu – Limitless Love* in Kumar, S. and Whitefield, F.: *Visionaries of the 20th Century – A Resurgence Anthology*: Green Books Ltd: Totness: 2006: p183

58. Butler, B.: *Living with Faith – Journeys towards Trust, Friendship and Justice*: Inspire: Peterborough: 2006: p119

59. Vanier, J.: *Finding Peace*: House of Anansi Press Inc.: Toronto: 2003: p59

60. Shortt, R.: *Rowan's Rule – The Biography of the Archbishop*: Hodder and Stoughton: London: 2009: p179

61. Ellsberg, R.: *All Saints – Daily Reflections on Saints, Prophets, and Witnesses of our Time*: The Crossword Publishing Company: New York: 2000: p326

62. Reddie, R.S.: *Abolition – The Struggle to Abolish Slavery in the British Colonies*: Lion: Oxford: 2007: p20

63. Durham, G.: *The Spirit of the Quakers*: Yale University Press: New Haven & London: 2010: p167-169

Chapter 4: Organisations

1. Kent, B.: *Building the Global Village*: Fount Paperbacks: London: 1991: p38-39
2. Hinton, J.: *Communities – The Stories and Spirituality of Twelve European Communities*: Eagle: Guildford: 1993: p49
3. Bartlett, R.: *Tolstoy – A Russian Life*: Profile Books: London: 2010: p376
4. Alexander, H.G.: *The Growth of the Peace Testimony of the Society of Friends*: Quaker Peace and Service: London: 1982: p19
5. Chryssides, G.: *The Elements of Unitarianism*: Element Books Ltd: Dorset: 1998: p75-76
6. Krieder, A & Yoder, J.H.: *The Anabaptists* in *The History of Christianity*: Lion Publishing plc: Oxford: 1977: p404
7. Bartlett, R.: *Tolstoy – A Russian Life*: Profile Books: London: 2010: p370
8. Gillman, H.: *A Light that is Shining – An Introduction to the Quakers*: Quaker Home Service: London: 1988: p39
9. Alexander, H.G.: *The Growth of the Peace Testimony of the Society of Friends*: Quaker Peace and Service: London: 1982: p3
10. Alexander, H.G.: *The Growth of the Peace Testimony of the Society of Friends*: Quaker Peace and Service: London: 1982
11. Finucane, R: *The Waldensians* in *The History of Christianity*: Lion Publishing plc: Oxford: 1977: p327-329

Bibliography:

Alexander, H.G.: *The Growth of the Peace Testimony of the Society of Friends*: Quaker Peace and Service: London: 1982

Allen, D.: *Mahatma Gandhi*: Reaktion Books Ltd.: London: 2011

Bartlett, R.: *Tolstoy – A Russian Life*: Profile Books: London: 2010

Brabazon, J.: *Albert Schweitzer – Reverence for Life* in Kumar, S. & Whitefield, F. (eds.): *Visionaries of the 20th Century – A Resurgence Anthology*: Green Books, Ltd.: Totnes: 2006

Bushrui, S.: Introduction to Gibran, K.: *The Prophet – A New Annotated Edition*: Oneworld: London: 2013

Bushrui, S. & Jenkins, J.: *Kahlil Gibran, Man and Poet*: Oneworld: Oxford: 2008

Butler, B.: *Living with Faith – Journeys towards Trust, Friendship and Justice*: Inspire: Peterborough: 2006

Carson, C. (Ed.): *The Autobiography of Martin Luther King, Jr.*: Grand Central Publishing: NY and Boston: 1998

Cato, J. (Introduction): *Mysticism – The Experience of the Divine*: Chronicle books: San Francisco: 1994

Chryssavgis, J. and Gallaher, B.: *Orthodox Meet in Crete* in *The Tablet*: London: 23rd June, 2016

Clark, K: *The Orthodox Church*: Simple Guides: London: 2009

Chryssides, G.: *The Elements of Unitarianism*: Element Books Ltd: Dorset: 1998

Cunningham, M: *Faith in the Byzantine World*: Lion Publishing plc: Oxford: 2002

Dandelion, P.: *The Quakers – A Short Introduction*: Oxford University Press: Oxford: 2008

Dear, J.: *Henri Nouwen's Spirituality of Peace* in *National Catholic Recorder*: Kansas: Oct. 17, 2006

Dear, J.: *Transfiguration – A Meditation on Transforming Ourselves and Our World*: Doubleday: New York: 2007

Du Boulay, S.: *Bede Griffiths – Modern Mystic* in Kumar, S. & Whitefield, F. (eds.): *Visionaries of the 20ᵗʰ Century – A Resurgence Anthology*: Green Books Ltd.: Totnes: 2006

Durham, G.: *The Spirit of the Quakers*: Yale University Press: New Haven & London: 2010

Ellsberg, R.: *All Saints – Daily Reflections on Saints, Prophets, and Witnesses of our Time*: The Crossword Publishing Company: New York: 2000

Encyclical Letter Laudata Si' of the Holy Father Francis on the Care of our Common Home: Vatican: 2016

Finucane, R: *The Waldensians* in *The History of Christianity*: Lion Publishing plc: Oxford: 1977

Forest, J.: *Living with Wisdom – A Life of Thomas Merton*: Orbis Books: Maryknoll NY: 1991

Forest, J.: Postscript to Hanh, T.N.: *The Miracle of Mindfulness*: Rider: London: 2008

Freyer, J.: *George Fox and the Children of Light*: Thistle Publishing: London: 2013

Gandhi, M.K.: *M.K. Gandhi - An Autobiography* or *The Story of my Experiments with Truth*: Penguin: London: 2001

Gascoigne, B: The Christians: Granada Publishing: London: 1977

Gibran, K.: The Prophet – A New Annotated Edition: Oneworld: Cornwall: 2012

Gillman, H.: *A Light that is Shining – An Introduction to the Quakers*: Quaker Home Service: London: 1988

Griffiths, B.: *The Golden string – An Autobiography*: Fount Paperbacks: London: 1979

Hart, D.B.: *The Story of Christianity – A History of 2000 Years of the Christian Faith*: Quercus: London: 2013

Hilliard, A. & Bailey, J.: *Living Stones Pilgrimage – With the Christians of the Holy Land*: Cassell: London: 1999

Hinton, J.: *Communities – The Stories and Spirituality of Twelve European Communities*: Eagle: Guildford: 1993

Holt, B.P.: *A Brief History of Christian Spirituality*: Lion Publishing plc: Oxford: 1997

Kavanagh, J.: *The World is Our Cloister – A Guide to the Modern Religious Life*: O Books: Winchester, 2007

Kent, B.: *Building the Global Village*: Fount Paperbacks: London: 1991

Kent, B.: *Undiscovered Ends – An Autobiography*: Harper Collins: London: 1992

King James Version: *The Holy Bible*

Kirk, J.A.: *Martin Luther King* in Kumar. S. & Whitefield, F.: *Visionaries of the 20ᵗʰ Century – A Resurgence Anthology*: Totnes: 2006

Krieder, A & Yoder, J.H.: *Christians and War* in *The History of Christianity*: Lion Publishing plc: Oxford: 1977

Krieder, A & Yoder, J.H.: *The Anabaptists* in *The History of Christianity*: Lion Publishing plc: Oxford: 1977

Kung, H.: *Tracing the Way – Spiritual Dimensions of the World's Religions*: Continuum: London: 2002

Linder, R.D.: *The Catholic Reformation* in *The History of Christianity*: Lion Publishing plc: Oxford: 1977

MacCulloch, D.: *Silence – A Christian History*: Penguin Books: London: 2013

Markus, G (Ed.): *The Radical Tradition – Saints in the Struggle for Justice and Peace*: Darton, Longman and Todd: London: 1992

Martin, D: Walter Wink, Theologian and Author, Dies at 76 in The New York Times (http://mobile.nytimes.com): 19ᵗʰ May 2012

McKitterick, D.: Cardinal Kim Sou-hwan – The First Korean Cardinal and a Campaigner for Human Rights in The Independent (www.independent.co.uk): Saturday 21ˢᵗ February 2009

Meddler, L.: *Thomas Merton – Activist Monk* in Kumar, S. & Whitefield, F. (eds.): *Visionaries of the 20ᵗʰ Century – A Resurgence Anthology*: Green Books: Totnes: 2006

Muggeridge, M.: *Conversion*: Hodder & Stoughton: London: 1996

Peel, M.: *The Last Wesleyan – A Life of Donald Soper*: The Cromwell Press: Wiltshire: 2008

Reddie, R.S.: *Abolition – The Struggle to Abolish Slavery in the British Colonies*: Lion: Oxford: 2007

Reed, C: Father Daniel Berrigan Obituary in The Guardian (www.theguardian.com): 2nd May 2016

Roberts, A.O.: *George Fox and the Quakers* in *The History of Christianity*: Lion Publishing plc: Oxford: 1977

Sellars, I.: *The Unitarians* in *The History of Christianity*: Lion Publishing plc: Oxford: 1977

Sharma, A.: *Gandhi – A Spiritual Biography*: Yale University Press: 2013

Shirer, W.L.: *Gandhi – A Memoir: Abacus*: London: 1979

Schumacher, D.: *Desmond Tutu – Limitless Love* in Kumar, S. and Whitefield, F.: *Visionaries of the 20th Century – A Resurgence Anthology*: Green Books Ltd: Totness: 2006

Shortt, R.: *Rowan's Rule – The Biography of the Archbishop*: Hodder and Stoughton: London: 2009

Starr, M: *God of Love – A Guide to the Heart of Judaism, Christianity and Islam*: Monkfish Book Publishing Company: New York: 2012

Tolstoy, L: *The Kingdom of God is Within You*: Wallachia Publishers: 2015

Vanier, J.: *Finding Peace*: House of Anansi Press Inc.: Toronto: 2003

Waite, T: *Taken on Trust (25th Anniversary Edition)*: Hodder and Stoughton: London: 2016

Walker, D.: *A Dangerous Priest* in *Church of England Newspaper*: London: 13/02/2012

Waterfield, R.: *Kahlil Gibran – Poet of the Soul* in Kumar, S. & Whitefield, F.: Visionaries of the 20th Century – A Resurgence Anthology: Green Books Ltd.: Totnes: 2006

Williams, R: *Where God Happens – Discovering Christ in One Another*: New Seeds: Boston: 2005

Yoder, J.H.: The Politics of Jesus (2nd Edition): Erdmans

Yogananda, P.: *Autobiography of a Yogi*: Self-Realisation Fellowship: Los Angeles: 2010

Appendices:

Appendix 1: People Profiled in Chapter 3

Armstrong, Karen

Baez, Joan

Bartholomew the First (Ecumenical Patriarch)

Bell, George

Berrigan, Daniel

Berrigan, Phillip

Brittain, Vera

Carter, Jimmy

Ceresole, Pierre

Day, Dorothy

Dear, Fr. John

Forest, Jim

Fox, George

Francis of Assisi

Francis, Pope

Fry, Elizabeth

Gandhi, M.K.

Gibran, Khalil

Griffiths, Bede

Hammerskjold, Dag

Hennacy, Ammon

Hodgekin, Henry

Huddleston, Trevor

De Hueck Doherty, Catherine

Jagerstatter, Franz

Kent, Bruce

Kim Sou-Hwan, Cardinal Stephen

King, Martin Luther

Kung, Hans

Maguire (nee Corrigan), Mairead

Maurin, Peter

Merton, Thomas

Nouwen, Henri

Oestreicher, Paul

Penn, William

Prejean, Helen

Ramabai, Pandita

Reeves, Donald

Romero, Archbishop Oscar

Sabbah, Michel

Schweitzer, Albert

Sheppard, Dick

Simons, Menno

Skobtsova, Maria

Soper, Lord Donald

Teresa of Calcutta, Mother

Tolstoy, Leo

Tutu, Archbishop Desmond

Underhill, Evelyn

Vananu, Mordechai

Vanier, Jean

Waite, Terry

Williams, Betty

Williams, Rowan

Wilberforce, William

Wink, Walter

Woolman, John

Yoder, John Howard

Appendix 2: Organisations Profiled in Chapter 4

Anabaptist Network

Anglican Peace and Justice Network (APJN)

Anglican Pacifist Fellowship (APF)

Archbishop Romero Trust

Baptist Peace Fellowship

Bruderhof Communities

Caritas Internationalis

Carter Center

Catholic Agency for Oversees Development (CAFOD)

Catholic Worker Movement

Centre for Action and Contemplation (CAC)

Christian Aid

Christians Aware

Christian Campaign for Nuclear Disarmament (CCND)

Christian Peacemaker Teams (CPT)

Community of Sant' Egidio

Council of Christians and Jews (CCJ)

Coventry Cathedral

Doukhobors, The

Ecumenical Accompaniment Programme in Palestine and Israel (EAPPI)

Elijah Interfaith Institute

Fellowship of Reconciliation (FOR)

Habitat for Humanity

International Association for Religious Freedom (IARF)

Living Stones of the Holy Land Trust

Mennonites, The

Mennonite Trust

Methodist Peace Fellowship

Molokans, The

Moravian Church

Orthodox Peace Fellowship

Pax Christi International

Pax Christi, U.K.

Plowshares Movement

Quakers, The

Religions for Peace

Shakers, The

Soul of Europe, The

St. Etelburga's Centre for Peace and Reconciliation

St. Philip's Centre

Tolstoyan Communities / Colonies

Tutu Foundation, The

Unitarian Peace Fellowship

Unitarians, The

United Reformed Peace Fellowship

Waldensians, The

World Council of Churches

www.ingramcontent.com/pod-product-compliance
Lightning Source LLC
Chambersburg PA
CBHW060404290526
45791CB00002B/604

* 9 7 8 1 3 2 6 8 7 4 2 6 1 *